Do You Want to Be Right or Do You Want to Have More Sex?™

DO YOU WANT TO BE **RIGHT** OR DO YOU WANT TO HAVE MORE **SEX**?
50 "Quickies" to a Happier Wife

Part of the
Do You Want to Be Right or Do You Want to Have More Sex?™
Series

Diane A. Ross
and
Kathryn Calhoun

Illustrations: Nelson Dewey, www.NelsonDewey.com

ISBN 978-0-9918113-3-5

This book is dedicated to husbands everywhere who love their wives, put up with craziness, and wonder why their best sometimes just isn't good enough.

Table of **Contents**

Disclaimer 11

Introduction 13

Quickie 1: Why you're driving your wife crazy 17

Quickie 2: Your wife is lying to you 19

Quickie 3: You Got the Brilliant, Sexy, Fabulous Wife? Uh oh. 21

Quickie 4: Your wife isn't a gold-digger, so stop wishing she was
.... 23

Quickie 5: How to read her mind 25

Quickie 6: Learn to speak her language in 3 minutes or less 29

Quickie 7: Advanced tips to speak her language – just 2 more
minutes! 31

Quickie 8: Defense (it can save your team but ruin your sex life)
.... 35

Quickie 9: How to kill the mood in 2 seconds flat 37

Quickie 10: This will instantly up your sexiness factor (and it's
actually pretty obvious) 39

Quickie 11: She's the princess, not the maid 41

Quickie 12: …And also not the nanny! 44

Quickie 13: Housework = Foreplay 47

Quickie 14: The questions you ask that guarantee no sex tonight
.... 49

Quickie 15: Scratch her back so she'll want to scratch yours 52

Quickie 16: You only spend 4 minutes a day with her, max 54

Quickie 17: Notice her (not just her butt) 56

Quickie 18: …But notice her butt, too! 59

Quickie 19: Listen (instead of waiting for her to shut up) 62

Quickie 20: Validate her feelings (even the crazy ones) 65

Quickie 21: Let the noise go by 68

Quickie 22: Leave your toolbox in the garage............................71

Quickie 23: Women are like elephants 74

Quickie 24: Ace your apologies..77

Quickie 25: Never criticize 79

Quickie 26: Take a dump...81

Quickie 27: Wife vs. mom: the ultimate showdown 83

Quickie 28: Your folks got downgraded from "immediate" to "extended" when you said "I do" 86

Quickie 29: What to do when mom is right 89

Quickie 30: Women need women 91

Quickie 31: How to make her girlfriends jealous 93

Quickie 32: Prove you're thinking about her when she isn't in the room 96

Quickie 33: If she has to ask, it's not romantic...........................98

Quickie 34: Sexy men don't stink..100

Quickie 35: "Practical" ≠ "sexy"...103

Quickie 36: Choose your battles (and this isn't one of them) 106

Quickie 37: How to give her the perfect gift 108

Quickie 38: The worst time to give the worst gift ever 111

Quickie 39: Another pretty awful gift you should (usually) avoid like the plague..113

Quickie 40: The secrets to planning killer special occasions 115

Quickie 41: Planning the ultimate romantic getaway...............118

Quickie 42: Being thoughtful will get you in the sack.............121

Quickie 43: Sex – the magic number 123

Quickie 44: The sex move that always flops 126

Quickie 45: Things not to say if you want to have sex..............128

Quickie 46: Your relationship bank account terms suck...........130

Quickie 47: 10-second sex tips 132

Quickie 48: One-minute sex tips 134

Quickie 49: 10-minute sex tips..136

Quickie 50: Foreplay takes time 139

Endnotes 143

Disclaimer

The use by you of this book (the "Book") is subject to certain understandings and the terms and conditions set forth below. By using the Book, you acknowledge that you have read and accept such understandings and such terms and conditions.

The Authors make no warranties or representations of any kind whatsoever concerning any information made available on or through the Book. The content of the Book is provided only as general information. The Authors disclaim all liability with respect to actions taken or not taken based upon such information or with respect to any errors or omissions in such information. More specifically, The Authors shall not be liable for any direct, indirect, consequential, special, exemplary or other damages of any kind whatsoever and howsoever caused.

The stories shared in this Book come from the Authors' own experiences as well as the accounts of others that have been shared with the Authors. Certain stories are fictional and for illustrative purposes only. In order to protect confidentiality, most of the stories and accounts have modified and the names of those involved or affected have been changed.

The Book is to be used for entertainment purposes only. If you require marriage and/or relationship advice, please consider seeking the advice of a therapist licensed in marriage counseling.

Introduction

Picture this: You come home from work and as soon as you spot your wife, you can tell something's up. She's giving you the silent treatment as she stomps around the kitchen, putting the finishing touches on dinner.

You've been here before; you know to tread lightly. So, you start with, "How was your day, honey?"

"Fine," she says curtly, hacking up a tomato as if she were exacting some kind of gory revenge. "You?"

"Oh, my day was alright," you say slowly. She doesn't respond so, to break this mysterious tension, you ask her again, "Are you sure your day was okay?"

"It was fine," she repeats, not looking at you.

"It's just that you seem... upset."

Finally, the dam bursts. "Oh, why would I be upset?" she says sarcastically. "Certainly not because I spent my day fighting with the kids and certainly not because I had to hang up your towel, which you left on our bed *again*! And definitely not because the dishwasher repairman never showed up and definitely not because of the unbelievable things your mother said to me when she called this afternoon..."

As your wife lists her complaints, you try to understand what's happening. She's obviously supremely pissed off, but why is she pissed off *at you*? All you did is leave one solitary damp towel on the bed; the rest of the stuff – the kids, your mom – isn't your fault. You're bearing the brunt of her extreme discontent and, even though you can hardly be blamed for the dishwasher repairman not showing up when he said he would, you somehow know that this fight is going to mean what it always means: *no sex tonight.*

This book is for every husband who's ever been left reeling after one of his wife's meltdowns and wondered to himself, *What just happened?* It's for the man who wants, above all else, for his wife to be happy but, somehow, seems to be missing the mark more often than not. It's for the guy who isn't getting as much action in the sack as he would like and wants desperately to connect with his wife on a more intimate level.

You're not alone. *Do You Want to Be Right or Do You Want to Have More Sex?* contains 50 "Quickies" – tips to spice up your marriage and your love life – that have been time-tested and wife-approved. The goal is to help you understand why your wife sometimes behaves the way she does and what you can do to navigate those storms safely.

Like anything else in life, when you don't have the tools that you need, it can be next to impossible to create the thing that you're trying to create. It's hard to put together a piece of furniture if you don't have the right screwdriver, and it's hard to build a successful marriage (one that includes a hot sex life) if you don't really know how to turn your wife on and, just as importantly, how *not* to turn her off.

Please note that this book isn't intended to replace marriage counseling or sex therapy; it's simply to help ordinary husbands who love their wives to restore some of the intimacy that they feel is lacking. The goal is to help you address and tackle some of the most common problems that husbands face in their marriages, but if at any point you feel that you and your wife need more specialized attention, please do not hesitate to seek the assistance of a professional.

Read the Quickies in order, or skim the book to find the ones that are most relevant to your individual situation. While some of the Quickies in this book build on some of the others, you can definitely glean helpful advice from any individual Quickie –

usually in five minutes or less (perfect for reading in privacy on the can!). Each Quickie contains real-life advice and actionable tips to help you on your path to a happier wife and a better sex life. There are also lots of stories, examples, and tips to earn brownie points to help you score big with the missus.

We hope you enjoy this book as much as we enjoyed writing it; but, more importantly, we hope that the tips you discover within are as beneficial to your marriage as they have been to our marriages. You have nothing to lose and everything to gain, including some fresh perspectives, a happier wife, a more harmonious relationship and, hopefully, a little extra wear and tear on your mattress. Happy reading!

Quickie 1:
Why you're driving your wife **crazy**

"Women use sex as a weapon."

Is it true? What does it mean, really?

When people say women use sex as a weapon, what they usually mean is that a woman *withholds* sex as a way to punish her man, as if she derives some kind of vile pleasure out of dangling something you really, *really* want just beyond your fingertips.

But guess what? Women don't like not having sex, either. Believe me: when a woman's not into heating up the bedroom with her man, it isn't because she just doesn't like sex. It isn't even because she just doesn't like sex with you. It's far more likely that she's just so tired and overwhelmed (especially if you have kids) that she's kind of forgotten how great it can actually be – seriously.

So does she really withhold sex as punishment? Yup, sorry – but it's not because she's trying to run you through with some kind of evil sex weapon. It's because she's trying to tell you something: she doesn't feel supported by you and it's snuffing out her flame.

"But I'm supportive!" you're saying. "I earn a great living, I'm a loving father, we take nice vacations together, I help out around the house, I remember her birthday, I take care of XYZ…"

Sorry, but even if you feel like you're doing everything you can to support your wife, if she's not into sex, it's almost always because she *feels* unsupported by you. That means that, while you may be trying to support your wife in your own way, what you actually need to be doing is supporting her in the way she secretly needs.

Women are kind of weird. When a man is frustrated from a lack of sex, he (logically) thinks to himself, *I wish I were having more sex*. But when a woman is frustrated from a lack of sex, she thinks to herself, *Why can't he be more supportive? Why is he so self-absorbed? He is driving me crazy!*

The reason women identify their own sexual frustration in this way is because their desire for sex is interwoven with their need for support from their husbands. It is practically *impossible* for a woman to get turned on by her husband when she feels let down by him – and the longer this goes on for, the harder it gets for her to ever think about her husband sexually.

In other words, if you want to get laid more often, you're going to have to give her what she wants.

How do you find out what she wants? The answer is eye-rollingly simple: Ask her. Pay attention to what she's asking you, as well. If your job is to take out the garbage on Tuesdays and you forgot – again – she's going to be pissed off; and the last thing a pissed-off wife wants to do is jump into the sack with her husband.

The good news is that you don't have to become a doormat or a 24/7 manservant. You just need to shift your understanding of support so that your wife is getting more of what she needs. As soon as that happens, you'll be getting more of what you need, too. (Who knew taking out the garbage could be so *hot*?)

Quickie 2:
Your wife is **lying** to you

Okay, maybe not *lying* exactly, but – as you may have already figured out – a woman does not always mean what she says… so stop taking her words at face value!

Classic examples include:

- "Fine."
- "Whatever."
- "I don't care; do what you want."
- "I don't need anything for my birthday; pay down the mortgage instead."

If your wife has just said, "No, it's fine, I'll clean up the kitchen myself," but then she stomps around slamming drawers and banging pots together, chances are pretty much 100% that there is a hidden message, a test, and a no-sex warning all rolled up in there. If you aren't sure, pay attention to her tone and body language. Those two things often communicate way more than her actual words!

Allow me to translate the message above: What she's really saying is, "You twit! I can't believe you would make me clean up all by myself after the nice meal I singlehandedly put together for you. I don't want to have to *ask* for your help; I want you to *choose* to help because you love me. If you choose not to help, that means you don't support me – and if you don't support me, there's no way I'll be in the mood tonight."

Harsh, right? Sorry, but that's how it is. For some reason, men tend to be a lot better at simply asking for what they want directly. Because they're so good at it, they mistakenly assume that if their wives want something, they will be direct, too. Unfortunately, women are horrible at asking for what they want – and until you wrap your head around this little fact, your marriage (and your sex life) will pay the price.

Why can't women ask for the help and support they want? The answer is because women feel that if they have to ask, it doesn't entirely count as help or support. A woman instinctively feels that if her husband really cared about her, he wouldn't allow her to stay behind in the kitchen alone to clean up after the family; he would just roll up his sleeves and pitch in.

This tendency is pretty obvious when you think about how much your wife does for you without you having to ask… in fact, she probably does it so often that it actually annoys you sometimes. But when your wife acts this way, it's her way of telling you that she loves you. Take a cue from that nurturing side of her and try to do the same.

Quickie 3:
You got the brilliant, **sexy**, fabulous wife? Uh oh.

So, we've been talking about how important you supporting your wife is to your marriage. Being supportive in the way your wife wants is a *huge* turn-on.

This is all the more crucial if you married a smart, successful woman who gave up on a big career for the sake of *your* career or for the children. Your wife has a lot to offer the world besides being a housewife and baby-maker, but she chose not to – for you and the family.

You might be thinking, *Well, she can't blame me for her choices! I didn't force her to be a stay-at-home mom; she wanted to do it!* And that's reasonable, but what you have to understand is that no woman wants to be made to feel like all she is good for is housekeeping and childcare, especially if she used to kill it in the workplace. Yes, she made the choice to give it up, but her sacrifice can be a ticking time bomb in your marriage if she doesn't feel appreciated and supported in the role she's chosen.

What often happens when a husband enjoys success outside of the home and his wife doesn't is that the husband becomes the target of the wife's dissatisfaction, even if she chose to be a homemaker. The husband gets to go out, earn a living, enjoy the respect and companionship of adults, then come home to a clean house, a hot meal, and children who are dying to see him. The wife has been juggling the kids' tantrums along with housework, appointments, bills, cooking, etc. all day long – and all for no paycheck.

The secret to not letting this imbalance negatively affect your marriage – both in and out of the bedroom – is to be extra sensitive to your wife's needs and extra appreciative of the work she is doing at home. Let go of your belief that what you do is more important because you pay the bills. Let go of the myth that your wife doesn't work as hard as you because she "gets" to stay home all day. If you can learn to genuinely respect and appreciate what she does *and* demonstrate that respect and appreciation on a consistent basis, your wife will start to feel closer to you and more loving.

Think about it: how sexy could your wife possibly feel after long days toiling as both nanny and housekeeper (French maid fantasy lingerie notwithstanding!)? The key is to help her feel sexier by cherishing the work she does and reminding her every day that you know she is still that smart, sexy, fabulous, independent woman – not just a boring stay-at-home mom.

By the way, these tips apply even if your wife does work outside the home. Statistics still show that wives and moms who have jobs tend to sacrifice more at work – including promotions and salary levels – for the sake of looking after their families. Do what you can to remind her those sacrifices have not gone unnoticed.

EXTRA BROWNIE POINTS

Compliment your wife sincerely. Worship the ground she walks on! Every woman wants to feel like a goddess, so go out of your way to appreciate the little, mundane things she does every day. You might be surprised how far a compliment like "Wow, you are so breathtaking when you're reading bedtime stories to the kids" can go!

Quickie 4:
Your wife isn't a **gold-digger**, so stop wishing she was

Oh sure, you're glad your wife isn't a gold-digger, but a lot of men unwittingly treat their wives as though they were.

How?

At the heart of it, it's really about you being a good provider. You earn a decent salary – maybe even an awesome salary – so your wife can afford to shop, go to the spa, have lunch with her girlfriends, be a member of that gym she loves, whatever she wants. You work hard for the woman you love, so why aren't you getting much love in return?

The simple answer is that women need more than a blank check to feel fulfilled. She married you because she loves you, not because you would be this amazing provider. In other words, she wants more from you than your money.

It's good news, but most men are hardwired to be "The Provider" for their wives and families. You make both the necessities and the luxuries possible for your loved ones – maybe even as the sole income-earner – and you understandably feel entitled to a little gratitude. So, when that gratitude comes in the form of a snarky, pouty, and/or demanding wife who seems to be withholding sex out of spite, you're angry. And hurt.

We get it. It seems unfair.

When couples get stuck in this pattern, their relationships – and their sex lives – inevitably suffer. The antidote is to redefine your role of "The Provider" so that it means more than bringing home the bacon. Your wife wants to spend quality time with you. She wants to be *romanced* by you. She wants to know that you value her contributions to your family life as much as your own. It's up to you to be "The Provider" of that attention and recognition. The truth is, you're never going to get the appreciation you want from your wife until you start taking care of her emotional and relationship needs, not just her financial ones.

In other words, *you are way more important to your wife than your money.*

If you aren't feeling the love from your wife, chances are it's because she isn't feeling it from you, either. It can be hard to be the first one to break this cycle, because neither of you is inclined to reach out to the other when you're feeling so unappreciated. However, since you're the one reading this book, we encourage *you* to be the one to initiate the change. Start giving your wife more than just your money; shower her with your time, your attention, your appreciation, and your love. It may take a little time for her to adjust, but once she realizes that your emotional (not just financial) support is here to stay, chances are she will respond with the appreciation and attention you need, too.

Quickie 5:
How to read her **mind**

Newsflash: women and men don't think alike.

"No kidding," you're saying. (Yes, we can hear the sarcasm from here!)

Fortunately, learning how to read your lady's mind is not as hard as it may seem. Here's how:

- Stop making assumptions. Don't assume you know what she's thinking.
- If you want to know, ask!
- Try to pick up on her clues (body language, hints, tone)
- Still don't know? Ask again!
- Then ask some more!

Asking questions is always an awesome place to start, but be aware that if you're getting answers like "fine" or "okay," your wife is hiding something and you need to do a little more digging to get to the real dirt on what's going on (see Quickie 2).

If your wife isn't being very helpful verbally with what she's thinking, there are two things you can do: ask clarifying questions and/or pay attention to her non-verbal cues.

Let's say your mom is coming to town and she and your wife don't get along that well. You've asked her if she's okay with your mom coming and she says, "Yes, of course, it's fine, she's your mom." But still your wife seems agitated, anxious, maybe even mad at you. Instead of taking her at face value, pay attention to her body language and general mood. Obviously she's upset, but what can you do?

Okay, it's probably not realistic for you to tell your mom to take a hike, but that doesn't mean you can't figure out what your wife is thinking. It doesn't take a mind reader to understand why she might not be looking forward to a thorny visit with her in-laws. So, if you want your wife to feel like you're on her side, now is the time to ask more questions.

This doesn't have to be rocket science. Start by telling her that she really does seem upset and that you're worried about her. She will appreciate your concern. If she persists in saying she's "fine," see if you can be just as persistent. Ask more questions. Give examples to show you've been paying attention (for example: "I know you said you're okay with this, but I see in your face that you look really down. I would love for you to just share with me how you're feeling").

The super-weird thing about women is that when they say they're "fine" or that they "don't want to talk about it," they actually aren't fine at all and they really *do* want to talk. Hey, it can definitely be annoying, but it's your job to trust your gut and hang in there until she does open up. It can take time, but if you are patient enough to see it through, your wife will really, really appreciate it.

If it all seems like too much trouble, consider this: a woman who has something stressful on her mind can actually be *physiologically incapable* of being interested in sex... and the best way for your wife to reduce that stress is to talk about what's bothering her. And if you're the one to help her stress go down, she might just feel *really* grateful [wink!].

EXTRA BROWNIE POINTS

Learn when to read your *own* mind and not rely on hers.
Examples include:

- "What do you want for your birthday?" (If she has to tell you what to get her, the gift won't mean anything to her. It's just how women operate. She wants to see that you are thoughtful and paying attention – more on that in Quickie 37.)

- "Where are the baby wipes?" or "Where are my dress shoes?" or "What happened to my lucky jersey?" (If it is something you can figure out and/or find yourself, don't enlist your wife's help until you've at least made an effort. She isn't your personal assistant.)

- "When's our anniversary again?" (Hey, if you're hoping to get a little more action in the sack, you seriously can't be asking questions like these! What could be more of a turn-off than the man she loves being so forgetful about something so important? If you're really stuck, ask your mom or dig out your wedding invitation.)

Quickie 6:
Learn to speak her language in **3 minutes** or less

Okay, set your stopwatch!

There are a lot of books out there that teach you how to speak your wife's language because – let's face it – sometimes husbands just don't have a clue what their wives are trying to say.

Hey, we wives really don't make it easy on our husbands, so don't feel too bad about it! John Gray, author of *Men Are From Mars, Women Are From Venus*, got famous by explaining how men and women communicate so differently that it often seems like they come from entirely different planets.

Since we only have about 2 minutes and 20 seconds now (unless you are reading really slowly just to prove us wrong!), here are some of the main takeaways from *Men Are From Mars, Women Are From Venus:*[i]

- Women need to talk things out. This can take a long time. Learn how to listen without interrupting! Be patient.

- Women need to talk things out (yup, it's so important we said it twice!). Learn how to empathize with her (as in, "Wow, your boss was a real jerk!") instead of offering solutions to her complaints (as in, "If you're so frustrated, why don't you just quit?").

- Women want to feel understood and cherished. You can accomplish this by listening to her when she speaks and asking questions when it seems like she's upset but not talking about it (see Quickie 5).

- Women need to talk things out (there it is again!) in order to reduce stress and feel intimately close to their partners. If you can make her feel like the center of your universe while she's talking to you, that will go a long way in enhancing other aspects of your relationship.

The reason that listening to your wife can take such a long time is because most women aren't very direct when it comes to talking about their feelings. This isn't because she's trying to confuse you; it's actually most often because she isn't 100% sure of her feelings herself until she has talked them through (strange as that may seem!). For her, talking is a journey of self-exploration – and it's one she's really hoping you'll join her on.

Quickie 7:
Advanced tips to speak her language – just 2 more minutes!

Got two more minutes to spare? That's all we need to round out your crash course in speaking your wife's language. This time, we're revealing the genius of Gary Chapman, author of *The Five Love Languages*.[ii] He talks about how there are five primary love languages, all of which can be spoken by men and women. They are:

- Words of affirmation
- Quality time
- Receiving gifts
- Acts of service
- Physical touch

In other words, you will feel most loved by your partner if she "speaks" to you in a way that addresses your primary love language – and vice versa. This is not to be confused with you "speaking" to your partner in your own primary love language! If you aren't speaking *her* language, she might not get the message.

So how are you supposed to figure out what your wife's primary love language is? First, think about the things that your wife does for *you*; that might be a good clue. If she is constantly trying to spend one-on-one time with you, "quality time" might be her language. If she is always buying you little presents, "receiving gifts" could be it. If she often grazes your neck with her fingertips or gives you lots of hugs, it could be "physical touch."

The other thing you can do is pay attention to what your wife complains about. If she is constantly nagging you to help out around the house more, that's a big sign that "acts of service" is her primary love language. If she complains that you never compliment her, her love language might be "words of affirmation."

Many people speak multiple love languages, but there is often a primary one that will be most important to your partner. In any case, make an effort to speak *her* love language instead of your own. If you are showering her with presents, but her love language is "acts of service," she won't get the message. (In fact, I can practically hear your wife saying, "Oh sure, he brings me flowers because it's way less time-consuming than power-washing the deck, which I asked him to do three bouquets ago!") If you are always telling her how beautiful she is, but her love language is "quality time," not only will she not get your message of love, but she might actually feel insulted that you will compliment her but you don't seem to actually want to *be* with her.

Making sure she *does* get the message is key to smoothing out your marriage, not to mention spicing up your love life. Figure out her love language now – and you can thank us later.

DIANE AND BILL'S LOVE LANGUAGE STORY

Diane here! Just wanted to share how much success Bill (my hubby) and I have had by taking a few minutes to figure out one another's love languages.

We read Gary Chapman's book, then we sat down to talk about it. I learned that Bill's #1 love language was "quality time." I learned that mine was "acts of service." Before we figured this out, we would fight all the time. Bill wanted to spend time with me and have long talks, but I would just get irritated that he wasn't taking care of my "honey-do" list. He was trying to show me he loved me by planning afternoon lunches or tennis matches, but I just couldn't see it. I wanted him to "stop talking" and "start doing." He wanted me to "stop doing" and "start talking."

(Seriously, it amazes me how dumb otherwise intelligent people can be about relationships!)

Anyway, then we made some minor adjustments to accommodate one another's love languages and, almost immediately, things started to improve. My appetite was whetted. I shared our success with family and friends, and soon they were seeing improvements in their own relationships. I was jazzed! Give this stuff a try; see if it won't work wonders in *your* marriage.

Quickie 8:
Defense (it can save your team but ruin your **sex life**)

One of the biggest complaints we hear from our girlfriends is how defensive their guys get. I mean, it's definitely a natural tendency, but defensiveness is a pretty surefire way to ensure a sexless night, so you might want to try to curb it.

If you feel yourself getting defensive even after reading that one little paragraph, that's totally normal. When people (not just men) feel criticized or attacked, their instinct is to protect themselves by saying, "Hey, that's not true and here's why!" In fact, there is a study that shows smart people can actually be *more* defensive than most because they are used to being right – so if you tend to get defensive a lot, congrats: you're a genius!

Having a strong defense can be an asset in a lot of situations, like when you're making decisions at work or the other team is on your five-yard line; but when you bring those tactics home with you, they can drive your wife up the wall – and not in a good way.

If your wife is asking you to do something (maybe for the umpteenth time) or giving you negative feedback (otherwise known as complaining), do your best to simply listen without getting defensive. If you are interrupting her and trying to prove that she is wrong for feeling how she feels, you're only going to escalate the situation.

Is it hard to stifle your defenses? Sure – but not if you know how. Here's one idea that can really, really help: when you feel yourself getting defensive, instead of giving in to those urges, try listening for the "truth" in what your spouse is saying, the part of her message that you could actually agree with, the one that may or may not be hidden behind a critical tone or unkind language. (This is an idea that came from relationship expert John Gottman's book, *The Seven Principles for Making Marriage Work*[iii] - worth the read if you can spare the time.) Here's an example:

Your wife is complaining that you got home late from work – again. She is practically shouting at you because the quiche is now cold. She is obviously very upset. You're feeling defensive because you truly did not mean to come home late; it's not your fault that the boss called a last-minute meeting or that there was a huge accident on the expressway. Truth be told, you would have much rather been eating quiche with your wife and kids than stuck in that stupid meeting and nightmare traffic!

Instead of defending yourself with your (totally legitimate) reasons, put on your detective hat and hunt for the truth in her message that you might be able to agree with. For example, maybe you could see that it would be frustrating that she expected you home at 6pm and you didn't get there until 7pm, or that she spent all that time preparing a nice dinner and now it's gone cold. If you were in her shoes, it's possible that you would feel the same way.

If you can listen to your wife and empathize with her perspective, I promise that she is going to calm down a lot faster. You might even get her to acknowledge that your lateness was not your fault, without you even having to point it out!

Then, once the storm has blown over, pop that quiche in the microwave and prepare yourself for a hot meal – and maybe even a hot night.

Quickie 9:
How to **kill** the mood in 2 seconds flat

If you're really hoping *not* to knock boots with your wife tonight, try any of the following foolproof phrases:

- "I'm sorry you misunderstood me" (in other words, "I'm not sorry, I just wish you were smart enough to get it")
- "I'm sorry you feel that way" (see above)
- "That's not what happened" (a variation of "I'm right and you're wrong")
- "That's not true" (another variation on the above)
- "No I'm not!" (Uh, defensive much?)
- "I was going to get to it"
- "Why are you always nagging me?"
- "I do more housework than most guys"
- "Nothing I ever do is good enough"
- "You have it pretty good"
- "I told you how to deal with it, but you didn't listen!"

What do the statements above have in common? Answer: each one is a defensive reaction that is 100% guaranteed to get and keep your wife's back (not to mention her knickers) waaaay up.

If you need a refresher on why defensiveness is so toxic to your marriage, go back and read Quickie 8. When you get defensive, you aren't listening to your wife's perspective. Even if your defense is legitimate, you still need to do your part and *listen* to what your wife has to say. Just as there is truth in your perspective, there is truth in hers, as well.

If you're stuck in one of these conversations because you messed up, just drop the defensiveness and apologize. It can be tough to swallow your pride here, but if you can say you're sorry and mean it, it can make all the difference in the world.

THE SQUASH APOLOGY STORY

Whenever Erica's wife, Stan, was late for their squash dates – which was all the time – he would use every excuse in the book to justify his lateness:

"I'm sorry, but you know how busy I am at work; my time is not my own."

"Hey, sorry if my providing for our family got me here a few minutes behind schedule…"

Although the word "sorry" was usually there, there was never a true apology. The real message was loud and clear: "I'm too important to get here on time!"

One time, Stan arrived for squash 15 minutes late and – no surprise – Erica was fuming. *Stan is late one time too many!* She fumed to herself. *He took up squash to spend more time with me and now he has to keep me waiting!?* she seethed.

That day, something amazing happened: Stan walked onto the squash court with a sheepish look on his face and simply said, "I'm so sorry I let you down and kept you waiting." That's it! No excuses, no blame.

Erica was shocked, but Stan's sincere apology caused her anger to evaporate, as if by magic. She took a breath and replied, "It's okay, honey – things come up."

And for their next squash date? He was on time.

Quickie 10:
This will instantly up your sexiness factor (and it's actually pretty **obvious**)

Chivalry is not dead, but if it is in *your* marriage, you should be doing everything you can to resurrect it.

Virtually all women swoon over gentlemanlike behavior. Your wife may say you don't need to open doors for her, but if you knew just how much she'd love you for doing it, trust us, you'd never leave her to get her own door ever again.

It's simple: Just mind your manners. Be a gentleman. Here are some charming but oh-so-simple ideas:

- Help her with her coat
- Drop her off at the front door before you go park the car
- Chew with your mouth closed
- Don't fart at the dinner table, especially in public
- Walk on the side of the sidewalk closest to traffic

You get the idea. Every woman wants to feel adored by her husband and, as you can see, showing your adoration can take almost no effort at all. These are small little acts that can make an amazing difference in your marriage *and* your love life.

THE BEST DOOR OPENING STORY EVER

Kathryn here! I wanted to tell you about a door-opening experience so awesome that I am *still* talking about it!

One bitterly cold winter night, my husband Fraser and I were driving to a jazz concert with a colleague of his. Fraser was driving and I was in the front passenger seat. When we parked at the venue, Fraser's colleague got out of the back seat and then just stood outside my door. I was a bit confused, but I just started to get ready to exit the car anyway; I undid my seatbelt, put my phone in my jacket, and picked up my purse off the floor.

Then the most *amazing* thing happened: I simply reached for the door handle, and right then Fraser's colleague opened my door! It turned out that not only was he standing there to open my door for me, but he was actually *waiting* until I was ready to get out of the car so I wouldn't have to be exposed to the cold a moment earlier than necessary! I was *floored*!

If you are wondering what the fuss is all about, just know that from a woman's perspective, that kind of above-and-beyond consideration is extremely, absolutely memorable and seriously super-charming. Trust me, these little things are a big deal! (And Fraser, if you're reading this, pay attention!)

Quickie 11:
She's the **princess**, not the maid

Think about the last time you watched a romantic comedy with your wife. The plot lines are all more or less the same: boy and girl fall in love, something happens to screw it up, boy (or sometimes girl) does a crazy, spontaneous romantic gesture to win the other back, they live happily ever after, the end.

Why is it that these completely predictable flicks do so well at the box office? It's because women swoon when they imagine a charming man sweeping them off their feet. We live for that mush!

Of course, in real life, there are far fewer fire escape marriage proposals and Empire State Building make-out sessions. Real life consists of dirty underwear, spaghetti sauce on the linoleum, and crumbs between cushions. Instead of your wife getting to have those princess moments she fantasizes about, all too often she's relegated to the less-than-glamorous role of maid.

Be honest with yourself, here: what share of the housework do you do versus what your wife does? If the two of you have adopted traditional gender roles at all, it's pretty much guaranteed your wife does more than you around the house. If that's the case, your wife may feel like just the maid – and you may unwittingly be treating her like one.

Think about it. How often do you just leave your breakfast dishes on the table before heading off to work? How often do you leave your dirty socks on the living room floor? How often do you leave your toothpaste spittle in the bathroom sink? It's hard for your wife to feel attracted to you if you're doing little things like these because they can make your wife feel like you don't appreciate how hard she works to keep your house in tip-top shape.

Notice that I'm not saying that your wife expects you to do 50% of the housework, so try not to give in to the excuse of "My job is to earn money, her job is to keep the house clean." More often than not, all your wife really wants is for you to not make her job harder. Pitching in doesn't mean you're coming home to a second full-time job. It just means taking one extra minute to put your dishes in the dishwasher, take your socks to the hamper, and wash your toothpaste down the drain. Little gestures like these show your wife that you appreciate her for the princess she truly is… which will make it that much easier for your wife to treat you like the prince *you* are.

(Note: if your wife works full-time, as well, it's only natural that she *will* expect you to do your fair share of the chores.)

THE ABANDONED BATHROOM STORY

Beverly was so sick of her morning routine, which consisted of picking up Harold's underwear, hanging up his towel, and washing his whiskers out of the sink in their master bathroom. One day, she just got fed up and decided to stop using their master bathroom altogether.

The days went by. Harold continued to use their bathroom, unaware that Beverly had only been using the main bathroom down the hall. Predictably, A full 14 days passed before he finally said one morning, "Hey, Bev, our bathroom is getting a little grungy, isn't it?"

Beverly replied calmly, "I don't know; I haven't been in there in two weeks!"

Okay, maybe it's not the best idea in the world for wives to set traps like this for their husbands, but it definitely illustrates how men can lose sight of how much their wives are doing for them "behind the scenes." Harold never noticed how much Beverly had to do to keep their bathroom (not to mention the rest of the home) clean; he only noticed when she stopped doing it. If you think you might have a little "Harold" in you, consider how that lack of appreciation might be harming your relationship.

EXTRA BROWNIE POINTS

Never make your wife pick up your dirty laundry off the floor again. She *will* notice and she may even swoon as if you'd whisked her away to a surprise weekend in wine country. Are you up to the challenge?

Quickie 12:
...And **also** not the nanny!

Those little bundles of joy changed your life in ways you'd never imagined, didn't they? Suddenly instead of just having one full-time job, you have two... only this time, instead of being compensated with a salary and bonuses, you're compensated with poop-filled diapers, giant temper tantrums, sleepless nights, crushing worry, run-up credit card bills, and a sex life that is on the verge of extinction!

Yes, yes, of course parenthood comes with its own unique set of truly amazing rewards, but it's no secret that kids are really hard work. If you work outside the home, that means that it's your wife who is probably doing the lion's share of the drudgework involved with parenting. According to Sheryl Sandberg, Facebook's COO who took the Internet by storm with her 2010 TED Talk about women's roles in the workplace, even when both husband *and* wife work full-time outside the home, it's still the wife who bears the majority of the parenting responsibilities – by triple.[iv]

We know you love your kids, but make sure you are honest with yourself about whether or not you are doing your fair share of the parenting. If your tendency is to settle in to your recliner on the weekends to watch sports and read the newspaper while your wife chases after the rugrats, know that you are part of a 1950s cliché that is officially one of the most unsexy qualities in 21st century husbands. (Friend, they are called "La-Z-Boys" for a reason!)

If your wife is picking up your slack, chances are she's resenting you for it. Many women treat motherhood as a 24/7 job, even if they work outside the home as well. Be sensitive to that by seeing your role as a father in the same way. Treat your time at home as time to bond with your children. You will never know what a turn-on it is for your wife to see you playing soccer with your kids in the backyard until you give it a try.

EXTRA BROWNIE POINTS

Think of something your wife normally handles on her own when it comes to the kids, then take the reins. For example, if she usually puts the kids to bed herself, offer to handle bedtime so that your wife can enjoy a bubble bath and glass of wine. Make sure to handle it all 100% yourself: find their jammies, read them books, the works. Whatever you do, don't bother mom; she's too busy falling in love with you all over again.

Quickie 13:
Housework = **Foreplay**

Men who clean are sexy!

There, we said it – and believe it or not, this is actually a scientifically researched fact.[v] So yeah, we get that you're busy with work and all of your other responsibilities, but if you can go out of your way to take the odd chore off of your wife's plate, she will *love* you for it.

If your wife has a running "honey-do" list, you're in luck because she's already mapped out a bunch of things she would really appreciate you taking care of: cleaning out the gutters, organizing the garage, fixing the leaky toilet, whatever. Instead of seeing that list as a bunch of drudgery you'd rather put off 'ill next weekend, seize the opportunity to show your wife that you appreciate and respect her by tackling those to-dos without having to be asked twice (or ten times).

If there isn't a "honey-do cheat sheet" for you already, feel free to get creative: sweep out the fireplace, replace some burnt-out light bulbs, or prepare a meal that freezes well (like chili) so that, on one of those crazy weeks where meal planning slipped through the cracks, no one will have to worry about dinner.

These are small gestures that require an almost insignificant investment of time, but will make a lasting impression on the woman you love. Every time you make the tiniest step to lighten her burden, you will touch her heart in a profound way. When she feels this type of support from you, the kind that says "we are on the same team" and "I appreciate how much work it takes to keep our life running like a well-oiled machine," she feels closer to you. That closeness can be the key to restoring intimacy in your relationship.

Please note that every marriage is different and that it may take some time for your wife to really acknowledge and appreciate your efforts. Sometimes we women get so focused on just making life "work" that it can take us forever to notice changes like this. Don't give up! Your wife's admiration will be worth the wait.

EXTRA BROWNIE POINTS

Cook dinner *and* clean up afterward! It's a rare treat for someone to not only be cooked for, but also to not have to do the dishes (Why do you think restaurants are so popular?). Don't ask me why, but a woman just can't focus on relishing that after-dinner cocktail with you if she knows the kitchen is in disarray.

To make these brownie points easier to earn, do as much of the cleanup as you can *while* you're cooking. Then, when you're done eating, all that will be left to do is throw the dishes in the dishwasher and the leftovers in the fridge.

Quickie 14:
The questions you ask that **guarantee** no sex tonight

Certain questions drive women absolutely batty.

You may have noticed this tendency when you ask your wife certain things and she reacts by rolling her eyes, stomping away in a huff, or giving you an icy death stare. (But seriously, guys, do you really need to ask where we keep the toilet paper? Have you *never* refilled the roll? Come on now.)

The questions that women hate can roughly be divided into the following three categories:

1) *Questions that make you look lazy, such as:*

- Can you get me a beer?
- Where is the remote?
- Honey, can you come here?!? (shouted from one floor of the house when your wife is on another)
- Where are my pressed shirts?
- What do you want me to get you for Christmas?

2) *Questions that make you look unhelpful, such as:*

- Where do we keep the broom? [Have you never swept the floor?]
- What time do the kids have to be at school?

- Can you please just do it yourself?
- Does the dog really need to be walked today?
- What's for dinner? [A better question that, incidentally, will answer the "what's for dinner" question without causing a hissy fit: "Can I help out with dinner?"]

3) Questions that make you look irresponsible, such as:

- When's my mom's birthday again?
- How do I work the dishwasher?
- I forgot, can you mend my dress pants before my dinner meeting tonight?
- When do I have to have this chore done by?
- Have you seen my cycling gear? I put it in the hamper.

Before we continue, let us just say that it isn't a one-off question that pisses your wife off, but a general trend of these kinds of questions. In other words, if you have to ask her once where the broom is because you're going to sweep the floor for the first time since she last moved the broom, that's awesome. But if you've asked once, try to avoid asking again. In a similar vein, if you're constantly asking your wife to do things for you at the last minute or to help you look for items you've misplaced, it's going to annoy her. Once or twice, no big deal, but if it's a pattern, it's a problem.

The reason women hate these questions is because they make you look like you rely on your wife for too much. The woman who said "I do" to you didn't say "I do" to remembering all of your appointments, keeping track of all your belongings, doing all the housework, etc. (unless you two had some highly irregular wedding vows!).

The other reason she hates these questions is because they make her feel like all of the responsibilities in your marriage fall on her shoulders and that she is married to child, not a man. A wife does not want to have sex with a needy, lazy husband. If you're guilty of letting your wife pick up your slack, it's time to show her you're still the smart, confident, competent man she fell in love with. For a woman, there truly is nothing sexier.

Quickie 15:
Scratch her back so she'll want to **scratch** yours

It goes without saying that you should have your wife's back, but it's still really important that you ask yourself if you are actually there for her when she needs you the most – just in case.

Think about some of the things that have been stressing out your wife lately. Maybe she's dreading an argument with your son's bully of a baseball coach. Maybe her sister-in-law has been making some snarky comments to her lately and it's getting her down. Maybe she has a high-stakes pitch meeting coming up at work.

The list of stressors in life is endless, but that's just part of being an adult. What *is* up to you is what you do when your wife is faced with something that's really bothering her. Your support means the world to her and can open up your marriage in ways you might never have imagined.

With your son's baseball coach, maybe you could offer to go with her to have "the talk." If she says "yes," be on time. If she says "no," have a bottle of her favorite wine waiting for her when she walks back in the door. If her in-laws are giving her grief, stand up for her. If she's prepping for a big meeting, tell her how amazing and talented she is, and how you just know she'll knock it out of the park.

Remember that when you support your wife, she can relax and, when she's relaxed, her thoughts more automatically and naturally turn to sex. When you *don't* support your wife, she feels alone and disconnected from your marriage... and that means that the very last thing she wants to do is fall into bed with you. For women, sexual intimacy and emotional support go hand in hand. You can't have one without the other... so if you can manage that "one," then "the other" may very likely fall into place all on its own.

Quickie 16:
You only spend
4 **minutes** a day
with her, max

...and if you manage more, you're above average. Congrats!

Seriously, it's hard to believe, but between jobs, kids, hobbies, TV, Internet-surfing etc. the average time married couples spend alone together every day is a measly four minutes.[vi] Since women need to connect with someone emotionally before they can connect with them sexually, are you really that surprised that your love life has dwindled?

Listen, buddy, your wife wants your attention, and it's unbelievably simple to give her more than four minutes of uninterrupted, focused time. For example, instead of burying your head in a newspaper or zoning out in front of your iPad every morning (hey, we all do it), sit down with your wife to breakfast and ask her about her plans for the day. Boom – five extra minutes of connection in the bag!

Because you are both so busy, you might find it challenging at first to get in more than four minutes sans kids, TV, and the like. However, do what you can to make it happen every single day. Yes, date night is great, but what you're aiming for here is regular, focused interaction with your wife day in and day out, not just when you can snag a sitter and get away once in a blue moon. A little bit every day will make a bigger difference than a grand romantic gesture here and there.

To make this transition easier, enlist your wife's help. Ask her to also find time to connect with you one-on-one every day. Tell her you miss her and you want to chat; she will love you for the gesture!

EXTRA BROWNIE POINTS

Axe one of your vices from your daily timetable and rededicate that time to your marriage. We are all guilty of watching reruns or hitting the snooze button one (or five) too many times. Instead, share that time with your wife. Those few extra minutes together can pay big dividends!

Quickie 17:
Notice her
(not just her **butt**)

Picture this: You come in the door after a crazy rush hour. You're starving and still fuming from what happened today with your crazy boss. Your wife has had a similar day (either at work or at home) and, as you walk in the door, she's swamped trying to wrangle the kids and dinner at the same time. The two of you are so preoccupied that you barely say "hello" to each other.

Sound familiar? If so, you're not alone. This is an all-too-typical routine that a lot of couples get stuck in. Life is busy – we get it.

But if you're stuck in a rut, it's up to you to unstick yourself! Luckily, this can be much easier than you might think. Start by giving her a hug and a kiss when you get home – even if she is barking out orders at you ("Set the table!" "Get the milk!"). Find her wherever she is in the house and wrap your arms around her, then tell her you missed her and you're happy to see her. This simple gesture communicates that you appreciate her and that you were thinking about her while the two of you were apart.

The important thing here is to *not* make this attention about her sexuality if your sex life is not currently in a good place. It's been said before and it will be said again: your wife needs to feel supported and appreciated by you before you have any hope of tapping into her sex drive. If you come up to her and just squeeze her tush and tell her how hot she is, there's a very real chance you'll offend her. Why? Because no woman wants to feel like a sex object while she is also feeling unappreciated. Your wife only wants to hear how irresistible she is *after* you have already met her emotional needs.

How are you supposed to know if you're meeting her emotional needs? Trust us, you'll know. Happy wives are more cheerful with their husbands, more physically affectionate, less critical, more patient, and more easygoing. When your wife's emotional needs are met, it will feel as though an unseen tension has suddenly evaporated from your home life.

One caveat: don't give up hope if your efforts to pay attention to your wife go unnoticed for some time. Your wife may not reciprocate at first simply because you're catching her off guard and she isn't sure what to make of your attentions. She may be too wrapped up in the stress of her own daily life that she isn't taking the time to notice you back.

Hang in there. In time, she very likely will notice your efforts, appreciate them, and reciprocate in kind. These kinds of changes don't happen overnight, but they are so worth the effort.

Quickie 18:
...But notice her butt, **too**!

It's pretty much a universal truth that men get sexier with age and women don't. (Color us jealous.)

Never assume that your woman knows how beautiful she is, even if you've told her before and even if she's prettier than all of her friends. Unless your woman is Superwoman, she *is* insecure about her appearance in one way or the other – gray hairs, baby weight that just never went away, wrinkles, sagging where there used to be no sagging, varicose veins... the list goes on and on.

Motherhood and/or middle age can make a woman feel very unsexy. As her adoring husband, it's your job to remind your wife how beautiful and sexy she is. The trick is to do it *after* you have appreciated her (see Quickie 17) so that she doesn't think you're just trying to trick her into sex. The true masters of this Quickie will wait until their appreciation has really sunk in *before* starting in on how hot and sexy their wives are.

When women are particularly insecure about some aspect of their physical appearance, chances are it's negatively affecting their perceptions of themselves as sexual beings. Your compliments about how she looks can go a long way towards dispelling those roadblocks to the bedroom. Here is how to deliver compliments like a pro:

1) Choose a part of her that you can compliment sincerely. If her butt is the size of Texas, pick something else or you'll

lose your credibility. (Women can smell insincere compliments from a mile away!)

2) Double-check that your wife feels appreciated and supported before you attempt a compliment about her physicality. Telling her she has the sexiest hips won't go far if she is stressed to the max about a huge fight she just had with your teenager.

3) State your compliment as a universal truth, not a subjective one. "Your legs are so hot" means "I think your legs are hot and nothing will convince me otherwise." On the other hand, the words "Your legs look hot *to me*," when fed through your wife's self-criticism translation machine, mean "Other people would never say your legs are hot; I'm just trying to make you feel better about yourself." (Sad but true!)

4) If your wife argues with you, argue back with emphasis. Yup, she is fishing for more compliments, but who cares? Here's an example using the same compliment from above:

You: Your legs are so hot.

Your wife: Ha, you *have* to say that! No one else would say I have nice legs.

You: It's not my fault if other people are morons. I'm just glad I have your legs all to myself.

Your wife: Ugh, I don't know, there is a lot more cellulite there than last year.

You: You're crazy! I don't see any cellulite!

Your wife: Trust me, it's there, and so are my disgusting spider veins. Do you think I should get them lasered?

You: Are you kidding me? Don't do a thing to your legs! They are the hottest legs in the world and I don't want you to change a thing!

If your wife giggles playfully at this point and smiles shyly, you've done your job. High five! (Note: this is the one time you will be allowed to call your wife crazy, so enjoy it!)

Quickie 19:
Listen (instead of waiting for her to **shut up**)

Most women love to talk – sorry guys, but you should get used to it!

However, the truth is that what women love more than talking is being listened to. Talking is just no fun if you feel like your message is falling on deaf ears. Wives especially are prone to feeling hurt when their husbands don't listen to them. Because being listened to is so important to a woman, she naturally feels that it's her husband's job to do the lion's share.

Listening is about giving your wife your undivided attention so that she feels close to you and supported by you. Listening means focusing on your wife's words as well as her body language and not doing anything else at the same time. If you are watching the game, fiddling with your smartphone, or reading while she is trying to talk to you, you'll likely be inadvertently hurting her feelings. If your wife starts to talk to you and you immediately put down the newspaper and look her in the eye, you will melt her heart.

But what if she's interrupting me? you may be thinking. *Do I really have to drop everything and listen to my wife when I am right in the middle of something?*

This is a fair question, and the answer is: "It depends." If your wife is having a nervous breakdown or she's really upset about something, you're going to look like a jerk if you don't stop what you're doing to listen to her. However, if your wife wants to talk your ear off about something less important and there's only five high-stakes minutes left in the game, you are well within your rights to ask her if she can wait until you're ready. It's as simple as saying, "Honey, I'm right in the middle of ABC, but I'll be done in XX minutes. I really want to give you my full attention, so can we talk about this then?" Then make sure you pick up where she left off at the time you promised.

The husband who has mastered the art of listening to his wife knows that listening is really about so much more than not talking. He knows not to interrupt, but to give little signals to prove that he is focused on what she is saying, such as:

- Asking questions to clarify what she's saying
- Asking questions about how she's feeling
- Making small noises of acknowledgment (such as "Hmm," "Oh wow," "Okay," "Mmhmm," "Really," etc.)

When a husband can do this, it communicates to his wife that he cares about what's going on in her life and that he respects her feelings and perspectives... both of which are huge turn-ons for the missus!

STORY: LISTENING IS SEXY

Kathryn here! I wanted to share this awesome little story about a girlfriend of mine:

One weekday evening, my friend and her husband were sitting on the couch enjoying a glass of wine. Their usual routine was to veg in front of the TV, but this particular evening, her husband had opted to leave the TV off and instead ask his wife about her day.

She started to tell him that her day was pretty ordinary, but then her husband dug deeper with questions like, "Oh, how did that incident end up playing out with your boss?" and "Did Theresa steal your parking spot again?" and "Where did you go for lunch today?"

These were all just little questions, but as my friend answered them, she confided in me that all of a sudden she became extremely turned on, simply because her husband was going out of his way to give her his undivided attention and really be present with her. I believe her exact words were, "I just wanted to jump him right then and there on the living room sofa!" (I wish I could give you more details, but my friend doesn't kiss and tell!)

Quickie 20:
Validate her **feelings** (even the crazy ones)

Put yourself in this situation: You come home from work and your wife is stomping around the kitchen in a serious huff. You walk in to greet her, but before you can even finish saying, "How was your day?" your wife launches into a tirade. "My mother stopped by for lunch," she begins, "but instead of thanking me for having her over, she whines that our coat closet is too cluttered and she can't find a hanger, then she tells me that the cheese sandwiches are lovely but we really shouldn't be eating so much dairy and that's probably why I haven't lost the baby weight. *Then* she tells me that we need to spend more time helping Stephen with his homework and that if he can't get his grades up, we should pull him out of little league. THEN…"

She goes on and on. You have just been blindsided by an emotional rant. What do you do?

a) Interrupt her and ask her to calm down.

b) Remind her that her mom is way too critical and she should just ignore everything her mom says and not take it personally.

c) Say, "Hey, what can you do? It's your mom," then tell your wife that maybe she should stop having her mom over for lunch if it upsets her this much.

d) Let her rant, then when she runs out of steam, tell her that it sounds like she had a crazy afternoon and that her mom put her in a pretty tough situation.

If you guessed (a), go back and read Quickie 19. (In a nutshell, interrupting your wife is never a good idea.) If you guessed (b) or (c), you are in good company but, unfortunately, those answers are wrong, too. The correct answer is (d).

The reason that (b) and (c) are not good answers is because they don't validate your wife's feelings. Even if you are trying to show you're on her side, you need to actually extract from your wife's message what her feelings likely are, then express that you understand them. In answer (d), the husband validates his wife's feelings by agreeing that the afternoon was crazy and that her mom was being hard on her. Bingo!

Here are a couple of other examples of how you can validate your wife's feelings:

> *Your wife:* My stupid boss made me stay late for the third time this week! I am not his slave!
>
> *Don't say:* Oh come on, at least you're getting the overtime. If you don't like it, just tell him you can't stay.
>
> *Do say:* Wow, he is being so disrespectful.
>
> ---
>
> *Your wife:* Our four-year-old was talking back to me all day today! She must have learned that garbage at preschool. I could have killed her!
>
> *Don't say:* She's just a little girl; don't be so hard on her. It's not her fault – they're like sponges at this age.
>
> *Do say:* You must have been so frustrated! It's amazing you were able to keep it together.

Figuring out what your wife's feelings are gets easier when you remember to give your wife your undivided attention when she is speaking so you can really listen to what she is telling you. The beauty of your wife talking so much is that you likely have time to decipher what it is she's trying to say. Best of all, you don't have to waste precious moments trying to figure out how to fix her problem; all you have to do is figure out how she's feeling.

Another trick for validating your wife's feelings: put yourself in her shoes (no matter how uncomfortable those high heels are!). Maybe you're feeling impatient that she's going through this same dumb thing *again* without doing anything about it *again*, but just remember that this is the woman you love; she is suffering and she is talking about something that matters deeply to her. If you can validate her feelings, you will be delighted to discover that her angst will disappear much more quickly – and she'll have you to thank for that.

Quickie 21:
Let the **noise** go by

Let's face it, listening is a lot easier when the target of your wife's dissatisfaction is anything other than *you*. But in reality, you're the one taking the heat a lot of the time, aren't you?

It seems to be human nature that people are hardest on the ones they love. Of course, this seems monumentally unfair. Sure, it's one thing when your wife has a legitimate complaint about something you've done, but what about when you're getting in trouble for something that is completely, 100% not your fault? Why shouldn't you defend yourself against those attacks?

Here's why:

Sometimes it's just better to let your wife's noise go by without reacting to it. For example, if she's whining that the kids wouldn't eat their lunch again, but then starts to blame you for never being around at lunchtime (i.e. while you're at the office earning a living), you might want to just let that pettiness slip on by without you taking exception to it.

Think about it: what would a counterattack accomplish at this point? Your wife is ranting and pointing fingers because she's upset about something, so if you launch into why she's being so unfair, what you're really doing is poking an already moderately antagonized bear. In many situations, her noise is not about you at all, so see if you can be the bigger person and just let that noise go by.

The best way to calm your wife down when she's being unfairly hostile toward you is to follow what you learned in Quickie 20 and validate her feelings. In the example above, you could do this by saying, "I'm sorry I'm not here to help more. The kids are really hard on you sometimes and it's totally unfair." If you can manage a response like this, you'll get to see how validating your wife's feelings can work almost magically to neutralize your wife's mood.

If you're getting stuck on the "I'm sorry" part of this message, it's likely because you're noticing there is an apology in there when, really, you don't have anything to be sorry for. Is it unfair? Sure. But what does it hurt to extend an olive branch? You have nothing to lose and a calmer, more loving spouse to gain.

Remember, when your wife is flying off the handle, try not to lash out in kind; a petty argument is not a good start to what could potentially be a very romantic evening, if you play your cards right by letting the noise go by. No matter how crazy your wife is behaving, it is always within your power to not escalate her negativity even further out of proportion.

THE CHIHUAHUA STORY

Diane here! I was out one day for a tennis date with a girlfriend. On the court next to us was a couple that, by all outward appearances, looked perfect: they were both good-looking, had nice outfits on, and were currently enjoying a nice, long rally.

Then the wife sprayed a ball long and immediately started yapping at her husband, "Why do you hit the ball so hard?! You need to remember your strength! Why wouldn't you place the ball to me?? If you want me to play with you, you have to be more considerate!"

This went on for what seemed like forever. She was completely overreacting! Honestly, she sounded more like a yappy Chihuahua than a human being.

What really raised our eyebrows was, when she was done, her husband calmly replied, "I'm sorry, honey." *For what?!?* I was thinking. *Your wife is a lunatic!*

My girlfriend and I continued to play, but this woman's nattering continued over on the next court every time she missed a shot. It was really annoying and we were feeling pretty sorry for her husband. Finally, at one moment when the wife was fetching a ball over the fence, I turned to this somewhat deflated hubby and said, "Geez, it doesn't seem to matter what happens, it's always your fault!"

He looked at me and said with a smile, "You've got that one right, but I'm used to it."

I couldn't resist replying sympathetically, "I guess if you argue with her, it means a big fight and no sex."

"You bet," he agreed. "That's why I've learned to just let the noise go by, because that's all it is, just noise."

What a smart guy, I thought. He understood that his wife's Chihuahua-like yapping was more about her insecurity than about anything he was doing. Sometimes you really have to ask yourself if it's worth engaging in the noise; your marriage will fare better if you can learn not to take your wife's noise to heart.

Quickie 22:
Leave your **toolbox** in the garage

A lot of men pride themselves on being "Mr. Fix-it." Leaky faucet? You've got it covered. Pilot light out? You're on the case!

While women appreciate having handy husbands, unfortunately your "Mr. Fix-It" side is very unwelcome when it comes to your wife's personal problems. What commonly happens is that the wife complains to her husband about something that's bothering her. The husband quickly spots the source of her troubles and offers a solution to eradicate her issues. Then, instead of the wife being grateful that "Mr. Fix-It" saved the day again, she gets even more upset.

Why does your wife react this way? Simply put, it's because your solution makes her feel stupid. If we run your reaction through the wife-translation machine, your solution translates to: "Look, your problem has a very simple solution! You must be too stupid to have thought of it yourself. Since the solution is so simple, your problem is actually not that big of a deal. You are overreacting and your feelings are totally unjustified."

This can seem like a pretty ridiculous extrapolation on your wife's part, especially if all you said was, "Why don't you just ask your boss to stop texting you after hours?" But trust us, she's not hearing your helpful tip; she's only hearing its latent criticism.

Although we are *sure* you didn't intend to criticize your wife or hurt her feelings, it's important that you understand why trying to fix her problems can be so hurtful. The biggest thing is that, when you offer a solution, you are essentially invalidating her feelings (see Quickie 20). Your wife wants to hear from you that it's perfectly understandable that she's upset. She doesn't want to hear a solution; she's smart enough to come up with that on her own.

"But what if she actually *asked* me for advice?" you may be asking.

Ah, this infamous trap can be very tricky to navigate. You know better than to offer unsolicited advice, but this time she's actually asking you what she should do. Now what?

First, realize that when people ask for advice, much of the time all they're really doing is asking for more time to vent their frustrations. Here's how to tell if your wife really wants your opinion or if she just needs you as a sounding board: Simply say: "Hmmm, I'm not sure. What do *you* think you should do?" By turning the request for advice back to her, you are sneakily giving her the floor again. If all she wants to do is continue ranting while you listen and validate her, she will take this opportunity.

If, however, she repeats her request for advice, it may be that she does actually want it. When this happens, do your best to offer a solution that includes validation for her feelings *and* does not contain any type of judgment. Here is an example:

Bad solution: Look, this doesn't have to be a huge deal. All you have to do is calmly tell your boss not to text you past 5pm. [This message can feel judgmental because you're implying her feelings aren't a big deal.]

Good solution: I can see how stressful this is; it can be really tough to stand up to your boss. Do you think you could ask him not to text you so late? [Much better! This message acknowledges and validates your wife's stress and offers a solution without making her feel like she's too dumb to think it up herself.]

Remember that just because you offered solicited advice doesn't mean that your wife will necessarily take it. Simply return to listen mode (see Quickie 19). That's all you have to do!

Not trying to fix your wife's problems is tough for a lot of men because, when you offer solutions, you are coming from a place of love. You don't want your wife to suffer with this issue any longer, so you try to support her with your advice. However, try to give the concept of "listening, not fixing" a go. When you see how much your wife appreciates you *not* swooping in to help, you will understand that, while "Mr. Fix-it" is a good guy to have around when there's a "honey-do" list to tackle, his sex appeal is pretty much zilch.

Quickie 23:
Women are like **elephants**

They say an elephant never forgets. Neither do women. (It sucks but it's true.)

Guys are definitely better than women at letting things go. Men get mad about something, they hash it out, then they forgive and forget. On the other hand, when a woman gets mad about something, it goes on her "laundry list" and will stay there more or less forever.

It's not really fair. We know! But what are you supposed to do about it?

Start by trying not to do things that you know bug her. If she's asked you to stop leaving the cupboard doors open after you get something out of them, just try your best to follow through. When things do happen that irritate your wife – as they inevitably will; you're only human! – just man up and apologize. She may not forget, but at least she should be able to forgive.

If your wife is stuck on a particular issue and keeps bringing it up like a broken record, it's probably driving you crazy and can feel supremely unfair. After all, you already apologized (right?). What else can you do?

First, recognize that the reason your wife keeps bringing this up isn't just for sport; it's because something feels unresolved to her and she's having difficulty moving past it. Even if it feels unfair to you, try to respect that your wife is going through

something and that it's your job as her husband to help her feel better.

Next, make sure you have apologized sincerely. A defensive response like, "Sorry, but it's not my fault that waitress was wearing such a short skirt! I couldn't help but look!" is not an apology. Something like: "I'm sorry I was looking at that waitress; that was really insensitive of me" will go a lot further. Even if the incident in question happened a million years ago, your wife won't be able to let it go until she hears a sincere apology.

Then, figure out what the two of you can do to move past these hurt feelings. After apologizing, you can simply ask, "How can we move past this?" Solicit your wife's help (because we *know* she loves to give advice) so that you are both on the same side, tackling the issue as a team, instead of it being wife versus husband.

Asking your wife to work with you is important because you want to communicate to your wife that it isn't fair for her to punish you for something indefinitely – and despite how women treat their husbands sometimes, they secretly find men who are doormats to be really unattractive. Although you standing up for yourself may elicit a tough conversation, hang in there; there are no greater turn-ons than self-confidence and self-respect.

Quickie 24:
Ace your apologies

Make no mistake: apologizing is a tough skill to master. Most people hate apologizing because admitting you're wrong or that you've hurt someone – especially a loved one – is one of the hardest things we have to do.

Apologizing is also hard when you aren't the only person to blame. When you're arguing with your spouse, it can be really tough to say "I'm sorry" while she's biting your head off, overreacting, nagging, or any number of annoying things.

Even if your wife owes you an apology, too, we challenge you to be the bigger person and get those apology wheels in motion. Just because your wife has something to be sorry about doesn't negate your obligation to apologize, so get it over with. (Plus, if you're hoping to get laid anytime soon, apologizing is your first step back into the bedroom.)

A lot of us really suck at apologizing because we feel a very natural urge to explain *why* we did what we did. The problem is that as soon as we start rationalizing our behavior, it undermines our apology. Here is how to deliver apology that will get results:

- Express your regret only when you can do so sincerely.
- Never use the word "but."
- Don't rationalize or make excuses for your behavior.
- Apologize for *your* behavior, not her feelings.
- Acknowledge how she feels.

Bad apologies (i.e. non-apologies) sound something like this: "I'm sorry you're mad, but I really didn't mean for you to take my comment that way." People – your wife especially – hate these apologies because (a) you're communicating that you aren't sorry you screwed up, you're sorry she's mad and (b) you're making excuses for why you said whatever it was that upset your wife.

Better apologies are much simpler. Something like: "I'm really sorry I said that; it was unkind" will go a lot further in disarming your wife because you are correctly identifying the behavior that upset her, validating her hurt feelings, and expressing your regret for it.

The only other thing you need to know about apologizing like a pro is to never do it unless you can be sincere. No apology is always better than an insincere apology. Wait until you've calmed down and can see her perspective on the matter before you attempt to apologize.

Quickie 25:
Never criticize

Diane here! On our wedding night, my hubby got a very strange wedding gift in the form of a two-word note from the father of a friend of mine. He had evidently slipped the piece of paper into my hubby's pocket earlier in the evening and when Bill (my hubby) discovered it, he showed it to me with mild surprise. It simply said: "Never criticize." At the time, we thought it was just a sweet (if naïve) gesture, but over the years we have come to realize that keeping criticism out of our marriage is the key to its success.

"Ha! No criticism *ever*? Impossible!" you're probably saying. (I know we certainly were!)

A whole marriage without criticism is admittedly next to impossible, but that doesn't mean it isn't something to strive for. Criticism will rot the core of your marriage; it honestly has no place in a loving relationship.

Before we get too far down this path, let's make sure to distinguish a complaint from a criticism. Marriage expert John Gottman defines them like this: A complaint is when you tell your spouse that she's done something you don't like. A criticism is when you take that complaint and morph it into something that is more like an attack on her character.[vii] Here are some examples:

Complaint: I'm really mad that you came home late without calling again.

Criticism: You are so selfish! You don't think about other people at all! How can you come home so late all the time and not think about the impact that has on other people?!

Complaint: I hate that we aren't having sex more.

Criticism: You're so cold and distant; every time you refuse to have sex with me I can tell you're just doing it to hurt me.

Complaint: I wish you wouldn't talk to the kids in that tone.

Criticism: You just don't think about how your tone is affecting the kids. I wish you wouldn't just say things without thinking them through first.

The differences are sometimes subtle, but can you see how criticisms are more harmful than complaints? Complaints make a legitimate comment about some kind of behavior in your spouse that you don't like. Criticisms attack your partner for some kind of perceived character deficit.

Both complaints and criticisms can cause heated conversations or even all-out wars with your mate. The difference, however, is that complaints are about the behavior in question, whereas criticisms actually erode the foundation of your marriage by deeply hurting the other person's feelings and communicating a lack of trust and respect. By all means, voice your complaints when they are important, but avoid criticism at all costs.

"But my wife criticizes me all the time!" you might be saying. In fact, there's a good chance your wife is criticizing you more than you are criticizing her – so what's the harm in retaliating every now and then? It's only fair, right?

If you have problems in the bedroom (or in any other room!), the cycles that are causing those problems have to stop sometime if you want to see improvement. Even if you're not the primary problem, your marriage will still benefit by you axing criticism from your repertoire whenever you can. If you want to, show this Quickie to your wife and see if she'll get on board, too. Either way, change has to start somewhere; why not with you?

Quickie 26:
Take a **dump**

… a mental dump, that is!

As disgusting as the metaphor is, flushing all of your negative, nasty thoughts is the key to being able to approach your wife for a tough conversation without risk of it escalating out of control. Even if your wife is still upset, your ability to remain calm will keep your conversation on track.

Taking a mental dump means getting out all of your nasty barbs, snarky jabs, and other unhelpful things before you tackle a difficult talk with your wife. If you need to apologize, respond to criticism from your wife, or bring up some thorny issue, a mental dump beforehand can do a world of good. That way, in the heat of the moment, you won't say something you'll regret.

There are lots of ways you can take a mental dump. Here are a few ideas:

- Go for a run or a walk alone
- Go for a drive (with or without blaring music)
- Find somewhere private where you can shout out all those nasty things (the car, the house when no one is home, your office once the workday is over…)
- Write a letter to your wife (then burn it lest she discover the evidence!)
- Vent to a buddy

When you take a mental dump that you really, really need to get out of your system, you'll feel lighter, more content, and more in control (much like an actual dump!). Taking this time to yourself is essential for keeping those tricky talks in check.

Of course, in practice it can be really tough to find the time for a mental dump. Between work, your wife, the kids, chores, etc. there often is just no time for you to be alone. If that's the case with you, feel free to ask your wife for some time and space when you need it. It's perfectly okay to say to your wife, "I am very upset right now and don't want to say something I'll regret. Let's talk about this in a hour/in the morning/after my run."

If your wife doesn't want to give you the time, stick up for yourself. Just because she seems to have gotten a little constipated herself doesn't mean that you have to hold *your* mental dump in! Simply reassure her that you want to have this conversation, but just not yet; then insist that you take the time you need for the sake of your marriage. She doesn't have to agree with you; she just has to understand that you *will* be resuming this talk in the near future. The good news is that, in the time it takes for you to have your dump, chances are she'll have cooled off, too.

Quickie 27:
Wife vs. **mom**: the ultimate showdown

Is your wife competing with your mother for your affection and attention? If there is any animosity or tension between the two of them, then the answer is a definitive "yes."

Don't bury your head in the sand about what's going on here: for the first couple of decades or so of your life, your mom was your #1 girl… until your wife came along. This transition can be really tough for a mom who is used to having her son all to herself.

As a side effect of your mom's struggle, your wife is getting put in a pretty awful spot. Many women feel like they can never live up to their mother-in-law's expectations. They also feel like their husbands often choose their mom's side over theirs. As the one they are fighting over, the onus is on *you* to prove to your wife that your mom's expectations and opinions are not as important to you as your wife's happiness.

Telling your wife that she is #1 in your life isn't enough; you have to actually make the transition so that your wife is always first and mom is always second. If you feel like you've tried, but the tension is still there, then try again. As the saying goes, actions speak much louder than words; if your wife still feels any anxiety where your mom is concerned, trust us, she isn't imagining it.

To get to the bottom of what's going on, ask your wife how she feels and what your mom does (or how you interact with

your mom) specifically that bothers her the most; she will appreciate your concern and very likely open up to you. Try to listen carefully to her feelings without getting defensive (see Quickie 8).

The bottom line is, simply stated, "wife before mother." If this involves taking a stand with your mom, so be it. Yes, it's not a good feeling to have to have that tough talk, but for the sake of your marriage – not to mention your sex life – avoiding it is simply not an option. After all, whom would *you* rather be sleeping with? Yeah – that's what we thought.

EXTRA BROWNIE POINTS

Say "no" to your mom the next time she wants something from you that would interfere with you romancing your wife. If your wife knows that you blew off going over to your mom's house to clean out the gutters so that you could make your wife a romantic dinner, she will melt.

Quickie 28:

Your folks got **downgraded** from "immediate" to "extended" when you said "**I do**"

We talk about "immediate" and "extended" when it comes to families. For a long time, your mom, dad, and siblings were your immediate family. Cousins, aunts, uncles, and everyone else, including your grandparents, were likely considered your extended family.

Now that you are married, you have your *own* immediate family. You and your wife are the heads of that family. Everyone else is now part of your extended family. What that means is that your priorities have to reflect that your own family members (i.e. your wife and kids) come first; all others (including your parents and siblings) come second.

As far as in-laws are concerned, common thorns in your wife's side may include: the "right way" to treat you; what kind of food you like; why she's raising your kids the wrong way; whose "honey-do" list you get to first; how she keeps house; and questioning her decision to work outside the home (if applicable). If any of this stuff rings a bell, well, the good news is that your families are pretty much the norm. The bad news is that if you want to start getting more action you-know-where, you can't just sit around and do nothing about this situation.

The simple fix is as follows: have your wife's back *first*. She and your children come before everyone else. As soon as you make this clear to your parents, siblings, and anyone else who may be getting in the way of your wife's happiness (and consequently your love life), things are going to get better. Also note that you might have this problem whether your wife and her in-laws actually "get into it" or not; oftentimes the husband is the middleman and the conflicts between wife and in-laws occur indirectly through (allegedly innocent) comments made to you.

Taking your wife's side is especially important *in front of* your mom/siblings/whoever is causing the problem. Not only does your wife need to know you're on her side, your extended family needs to know that *she* knows you're on her side. (Whew! Did you catch that?) Your wife will be proud of you for standing up for her – and that pride can go a looooong way.

Yup, that might mean that there is a showdown between you and your mom or you and your sister in your future. Too bad. The sooner you man up and stick to your guns, the sooner everyone will get the picture and you can move on to greener pastures.

STORY: THE GREAT SKIPPY SCREW-UP

Sarah and Terrence had gotten Skippy when he was just a puppy. He was the sweetest little dog: well trained, not too big, hypoallergenic. When Skippy was at home, Sarah and Terrence would let him sleep at the foot of their bed at night and play fetch with him in the yard during the day.

The problem was when Sarah, Terrence, and Skippy would go to visit Terrence's family. Terrence's mom wasn't big on dogs and there had been some catty quips exchanged in the past. So this coming trip, Sarah decided she would head off the issue at the pass by speaking to Terrence about it.

"We need to be on the same page," she said. "I don't want your mom to make Skippy stay outside all the time, especially at night. He isn't a farm dog."

"Sure," Terrence replied. "That sounds good."

Sarah was delighted to have Terrence on her side, but then something terrible happened: When they got to his mom's house for their visit, Terrence's mom said, "Okay, that varmint goes outside! He's not bringing fleas into my clean house!"

Sarah looked at Terrence, who was squirming. Then, after a few moments of stammering, Terrence quietly replied, "Uh, okay, mom." And out Skippy went.

Needless to say, Sarah was furious. When she interrogated him, Terrence begrudgingly admitted that he had never talked to his mom about it, hoping that she just wouldn't make it an issue this time. Of course, she *did* make it an issue *and* she got her way. Then Sarah and Terrence spent their vacation on pins and needles and Skippy shivered through the nights.

The lesson here is to really communicate with one another so that you're both on the same page, but also to not go back on your word just because you're in the hot seat. Sure, you don't want to have an argument with your mom, but if you don't help your wife fight her battles with your family, *you* are the one who is going to lose.

Quickie 29:
What to do when **mom is right**

Okay, so now you realize how absolutely critical it is that you have your wife's back and always take her side versus your mom (or anyone else). But what happens when your mom (or other person) raises an issue and you happen to agree with her?

This can be a veritable bear trap for the husband who understands the importance of having his wife's back, but also appreciates the validity of a suggestion made by his mom. How are you supposed to deal with this situation?

The key to getting out of this as unscathed as possible is to bring the issue to your wife's attention without bringing your mom into equation *at all*. Choose a neutral time and place (e.g. not when you're over for dinner at mom's), then simply raise the issue as if you had thought of the idea all on your own.

If your wife suspects you're just parroting your mom, there are two things to do: First, make sure you actually believe what you're saying and aren't, in fact, simply parroting your mom; second, explain to your wife that the issue at hand is about *you*, not about what your mom thinks. If she freaks out anyway, well, try Quickie 21 (let the noise go by). Once the storm has passed, you can remind her that this issue is still important to you and you would like to revisit it once you both have had time to mull it over.

The reason it's so important to take ownership of ideas your mom brings up is because it is very common for wives to feel ganged up on by their in-laws. In other words, suggestions from your mom can feel an awful lot like hurtful criticism and judgment, even if they are well intended. And if your wife feels that you're part and parcel of the people doing the ganging up, it is going to make her resentful and bitter towards you. She might as well hang a sign on the bedroom door that says "Closed for Business."

We've said it before, we'll say it again: your wife needs to feel that you're on her side *before* she can feel any other good things towards you. So, even if your mom has a really worthwhile suggestion for a change you and your wife should make, proceed with extreme caution because here's the truth: mama's boys are *not* sexy – not even the teeniest, tiniest bit.

Quickie 30:
Women **need** women

If you find certain qualities about your wife tedious, like her over-nurturing tendencies or her ability to tell the longest possible version of even the most mundane of stories, guess what? You're not alone. At any given moment, some guy somewhere is wondering, *What is she saying, and when will it stop?!?*

Don't ignore the fact that women need other women to talk to, spend time with, and just generally be girly with. Even if your wife is swamped every day with the house and/or the kids and/or work, take the initiative to help her carve out time to spend with her girlfriends. This is important for your wife because when she is in the company of women, she gets to be with other people who also naturally love to talk and listen. She can chat and vent and explore every nook and cranny of her feelings with someone other than you.

Doing so is great for your sanity because it lets you off the hook in terms of being her only support system and having to listen to every single syllable she utters. It can also give you a much-needed break to do the things you want to do (like maybe hang out with the guys or just read a book in blissful silence).

Your wife having girl time is also really good for your marriage as a whole. The two of you are individuals with individual needs that cannot possibly *all* be met by one another. When you spend time apart, you honor the fact that you have separate interests. You also give yourselves an opportunity to miss each other and appreciate one another's company. It can be just the thing to inject a little bit of renewed interest in spending time together; after all, absence *does* make the heart grow fonder!

When your wife comes back from hanging out with her girlfriends, she will be refreshed, invigorated, and likely very happy to see you (as long as she isn't coming home to a pigsty). She'll also feel a lot more in touch with herself and, when she's more in touch with herself, she's usually also more inclined to "get in touch with you."

Quickie 31:
How to make her girlfriends **jealous**

Okay, now you are aware of just how important "girl time" is for your wife. You also know how it can work wonders in your marriage.

Encouraging your wife to take time out of her crazy schedule to spend with her girlfriends will earn you some serious brownie points, but there's actually something more you can do to make her feel so lovey-dovey that she starts out her girly gab session with, "My husband is so sweet! You won't believe what he did for me…"

All you have to do to guarantee your wife says such awesome things about you is to simply hold down the fort while she is gone. Don't let her come back to your dinner dishes; instead wash them and put them away. Don't make her come home to kids who should have been in their PJs 45 minutes ago; handle the bedtime routine yourself. If you really want to "wow" her, do a little unexpected extra cleaning, just because. She will notice and she will be impressed! Then, the next time it's girls' night out, your amazingness will be the center of attention.

The reason you want to do these things is because your wife needs to feel that life can carry on just fine in her absence. Think of it this way: if you leave for a week on a business trip, how do you feel when nothing gets done around the office without you there? Probably a little stressed to be coming back to a mountain of work. You might even be somewhat annoyed at your colleagues that they didn't pick up more of the slack.

It's the same thing for your wife. If she feels it's okay for her to take time out once in awhile, without having to come home to chores that, really, should have been done in her absence, then those time-outs will be that much more refreshing. Remember, when she feels refreshed by "girl time," it means your wife will more often be the best version of herself, the one you fell in love with and got down on one knee for.

The *other* reason this Quickie is so crucial is because when your wife gushes about your sweetness and support to her girlfriends, she invariably gets replies like: "Awww! You are so lucky!" and "I am so jealous! I wish *my* husband were half as amazing as yours." Every woman wants to be able to boast about how great her husband is – and when your wife hears her girlfriends' envious replies (as opposed to, "Ugh! He did what?! What a jerk!"), it reminds her that she *is* lucky and that you *are* amazing. And that helps her to fall in love with her man all over again.

EXTRA BROWNIE POINTS

To *really* make her girlfriends jealous so they can't stop telling your wife how lucky she is to have you, try this little trick: Help your wife out by making or buying something she can take with her to girls' night. If your wife shows up with a brownie plate or margarita fixings courtesy of her man – *and* her man can keep the house in order while she's out – don't be surprised if she drags you to the bedroom the second she walks back through the door.

Quickie 32:

Prove you're **thinking** about her when she **isn't** in the room

The *New Oxford American Dictionary* defines romance as "a feeling of excitement and mystery associated with love."[viii]

Boooooring. What does that even mean, anyway? A definition like that is certainly not going to help the romantically challenged among us score points in that department.

We prefer to define romance as "showing your wife you're thinking about her when she isn't in the room." In other words, romance is all about making little gestures that prove that your wife was on your mind even though the two of you weren't together at the time.

Here are a few examples of what we're talking about:

- When picking her up from the airport, arrive with an "I missed you" card and have her favorite beverage waiting for her in the car (non-alcoholic, unless you want to get pulled over!).

- Pick up her favorite dessert or a fun appetizer (like a plate of fancy olives and cheeses) on your way home from work.

- Surprise her with everything she needs to take a nice bath (just ask the lady who works at the drugstore to help you).

- Give her a gift certificate for a mani/pedi or a massage, just because.

- Buy a packet of sticky notes, write compliments on them, then hide them in places that will catch her by surprise (inside a cupboard door, on the milk carton, in her gym bag, on her steering wheel, in her nightstand…)

- Pick up her favorite bottle of wine for dinner – not *your* favorite, but *hers*.

As you can see, these are pretty small gestures that take hardly any time at all for you to execute, but they will mean a whole lot to your wife. Women love to be cherished by their husbands; when they feel cherished they are a lot more open to giving back to their husbands in more intimate ways. If you can pull off a little surprise gesture of romance (more than once in a blue moon!), you'll be scoring some serious points.

Quickie 33:
If she has to **ask**, it's **not** romantic

As you may have noticed, it's not uncommon for wives (maybe even *your* wife!) to complain to their husbands that they aren't romantic enough.

These complaints are often problematic and confusing for guys because they think to themselves, *If she wants me to do something for her, why won't she just ask me? I am happy to help out however I can, but I am not a mind reader!*

This is a fair observation, except for one thing (and it's a biggie): women instinctively feel that if they have to ask you to do romantic things for them, then the very asking nullifies the romance points you could have earned. Put simply, if she has to ask, it's not romantic.

Why? Well, unfortunately, the answer is one of those great unknown mysteries of life… but trust us, that's how it works. (This phenomenon explains why your wife was unimpressed the last time you brought home a box of chocolates after getting into a fight about how you're not romantic enough.) If you want to score points in the romance department, there's no other way around it: you must figure out how to be romantic without asking your wife.

Luckily, most wives will leave you all kinds of hints, like when she says, "This is a nice merlot, honey, but it's been a long time since we got that pino grigio that I love." Or if she complains that her feet are killing her, give her a foot rub. This does not have to be complicated! The goal is simply to show that you're paying attention to her needs.

Note: if you have a long history of being unromantic and your wife has an equally long history of complaining to you about it, you can expect that your romantic gestures will take a little while to really hit home. This is simply because it can take time for your wife to realize that you're doing these things because you want to romance her, not just because you're sick of her complaining. Keep at it! Your efforts *will* pay off!

For more romantic ideas, be sure to flip through this book. You'll find lots of inspiration in its pages. Also, don't be shy about asking your friends' wives or even your wife's girlfriends. You aren't cheating by asking someone else – you just can't ask your wife!

Quickie 34:
Sexy men **don't** stink

This Quickie is all about reminding you that, sometimes, the best way to turn your wife on is simply to avoid turning her *off*.

If you have stinky pits at the end of the day and you crawl into bed to snuggle with your wife, chances are your efforts are not going to pay off. After all, it's pretty tough to make out and hold your breath at the same time!

Seriously, hygiene is a basic but important component of turning your wife on. It can be really easy to let those things slip after years of marriage, but they are just as important now as they were when you were first trying to impress her with your charm and good looks.

Take a moment now to remember all the little hygiene-related activities you took care of when you and your wife first started dating. Your probably wouldn't have been caught dead taking her to the movies if you hadn't showered or shaved in two days, so what makes you think she'd be into that now?

Here is a list of personal care to-dos you should be dealing with (bear with us here; you might be committing a hygiene crime and not even know it!):

- Shower as often as necessary so that you don't stink, especially when your wife is in very close proximity to you (i.e. in bed). Shower before bed if necessary!

- Shave! Most women love a smooth face. If you have facial hair, make sure it's neat.

- Deal with hair on any part of your body that grosses your wife out. If you have a veritable rainforest growing on your back or chest hairs poking out of your shirt collar and your wife hates it, do something about it.

- Keep your nether region maintained! If you want your wife to pay attention to your "bits," make sure she doesn't have to struggle to find them by wading through a jungle of unkempt curlies. Yuck.

- Choose a deodorant, soap, cologne, and aftershave that your wife likes. She is the one who has to smell you, after all!

- Don't try to get too many wears out of any kind of clothing. Once they smell, they smell. Wear something clean.

- Trim those wayward nose hairs and ear hairs, if you have them.

- If your eyebrows are scraggly, don't be shy about tweezing. You don't have to have a perfectly manicured look, but if there are any weird ones sticking out in odd directions or you have a unibrow, deal with it.

Taking pride in your appearance is not only good for your self-confidence (which, by the way, is the ultimate turn-on), but it also subtly says to your wife, "I want to look good for you." When you're shaved, showered up, sporting clean clothes, and wearing an aftershave she loves, what woman wouldn't want to take you out and show you off (not to mention have some fun under the sheets with you later)?

EXTRA BROWNIE POINTS

Try to keep a modicum of personal hygiene mystery in your marriage. Remember how you would have died if your wife had heard you so much as fart on your first date? Let's try to keep a little of that sentiment alive now: Don't clip your toenails in the living room or trim your pubic hair while your wife is in the bathroom. Be selective about asking her to pop the zits on your back or holding up your socks and saying, "Do these smell clean?"

Quickie 35:
"Practical" ≠ "sexy"

Call us shallow, but women care what their men look like! (Hey, you love it when your wife dresses up for you, right?)

Just because you're married doesn't mean you don't have to make an effort anymore to look half-decent. Since your appearance still matters, it's important to remember that "comfortable" does not equal "sexy." "Practical" does not equal "sexy." "Sweatpants on date night" does not equal "sexy."

So, what *is* sexy to your wife? This is an easy one: just let her tell you. If you're wearing something that she hates, believe us, she will let you know. Same goes for the times when you're wearing something she loves. If she says you look good, believe her. The only woman you care about impressing is your wife.

The best way to wear things that your wife loves is to let her help you pick out your clothes. A lot of women love to play dress-up with their husbands. So, if you need some new dress shirts, shoes, or whatever, ask her to come along with you and listen patiently to her opinion (which she will inevitably give – constantly).

We're not saying you have to wear things that you feel really uncomfortable in; we're just saying that it's a good idea to have your wife involved in the decision-making process. Having your wife on board will help you strike a balance between what's comfortable and what's fashionable. A lot of women are sick to death of their husbands' whining and excuses about how they "just want to be comfortable." There is a *lot* of comfortable clothing out there that also happens to not make you look like a nerd, so try to keep an open mind.

Listen, this may sound harsh, but part of the reason your clothing choices matter to your wife is because she doesn't want to be embarrassed by you in public. Getting defensive about this desire (for example by calling her "petty" or "insecure" or insisting you'll whatever you darn well please) is only the answer if you would prefer to be frozen out of the bedroom for the next several nights.

Again, this might sound shallow, but if you're wearing the wrong tie with an ill-fitting shirt or you've got white socks on with black dress shoes, you're probably going to offend your wife's sense of style. Sure, it would be fabulous if she could just let stuff like that roll off her back, but guess what? She can't. Get over it. It's just not worth your energy (see Quickie 36).

Think of it this way: You like lingerie, right? Well, sleazy animal-print thongs notwithstanding, there really isn't much in the way of men's lingerie for your wife to drool over. What you wear *every day* is the closest thing, so it's really in your best interest to wear outfits that your wife thinks you look seriously sexy in.

Quickie 36:

Choose your **battles** (and this isn't one of them)

If your wife is like most wives, she probably has a lot of opinions about what you wear. And, if you're like most husbands, you may occasionally find yourself in hot water for resisting your wife's critiques on your apparel choices.

We can understand why you would prefer to wear whatever the heck you want. However, this is one of those instances when it really comes down to choosing your battles. When you get defensive about clothing choices that your wife hates, you should know that those arguments are the furthest thing from foreplay that there is.

Think about it: sexual attraction obviously has a purely physical component. If it didn't, we would never think movie stars or perfect strangers were sexy. Sure, the *love* that exists between a husband and wife is about something much deeper than physical appearance, but *sexual attraction* is an awful lot about how a person looks.

So, the next time you consider getting into a fight with your wife over whether or not you should wear your 20-year-old stinky sandals to the neighbor's barbecue or if it's okay to wear jeans and sneakers together, take a deep breath and ask yourself, *Is this worth it?*

(Hint: the answer is a big fat "no!")

When your wife is getting on your case for your clothing choices, begging you to throw out your favorite pit-stained t-shirt, or complaining that your favorite cologne smells like garbage, do your best to listen to her point of view. When your wife brings stuff like this up, she is essentially saying to you (kindly or not), "I want to be turned on by how good you look and how sexy you smell." That is a request that you won't regret honoring!

THE STORY OF THE YELLOW HAT

One hot summer day, before heading to the beach, Andrea's husband Paul emerged from their cottage wearing a sunshine-yellow hat. We are not talking a ball cap, here, or even a panama hat. We are talking an extremely ample Tilley-type hat, one with a very wide, very floppy brim.

Paul looked beyond pleased with himself, but Andrea was horrified. "Where on earth did you get that hat?" she cried. "You have to take it off right now!"

"No!" protested Paul. "It's SPF50! Look how much shade it gives me! It's protecting my head and most of my torso from the sun! This is the perfect, most practical beach hat of all time! And check out the chin strap – it won't fall off when we're playing beach volleyball!"

Andrea could only picture the stares they would inevitably be getting once they were at the beach. "Listen here," she said, "if you ever want to have sex with me again, you will not wear that hat out in public!"

Was it the kindest way for Andrea to express her opinion? Probably not – but the next day, guess where she found that hat? At the top of the "giveaway" pile in the garage. Paul is one smart husband for choosing his battles *and* choosing not to get defensive over something as trivial as a floppy, unflattering yellow hat.

Quickie 37:
How to give her the **perfect** gift

Uh oh, another birthday/Christmas/Valentine's Day/Mother's Day/anniversary is just about upon you... *What* are you going to get your wife?

It can be really hard to know what kind of gift will knock your wife's socks (and pants!) off. It gets even trickier when you follow the golden rule of giving gifts to women, which is *never ask her what she wants you to buy for her.* This is important because if you have to ask her, then it won't be a great gift. The most perfect gift in the world instantaneously becomes a letdown if she had to tell you to get it for her.

If you are a guy who usually relies on your wife to just tell you what she wants, now is the time to distinguish yourself from the herd by choosing to use gift-giving occasions as a way to *surprise* your wife with how thoughtful, attentive, and romantic you are. Don't be like a lot of men we know whose wives not only tell them what to get, but whose wives also shop for, purchase, and wrap their own gifts. Some women we know even pick up the card themselves and hand it to their hubbies to sign – how *very* thoughtful (insert giant eye-rolling here).

Does being the kind of guy who can pick out a perfect gift seem impossible? It doesn't have to be. Here are some surefire tips to surprise your wife with amazing presents:

- Think about potential gift ideas year-round, not just two days (or two hours) before the big day. Keep a running list on your smartphone, so whenever an ingenious idea pops into your head, you won't forget it. Then, when it's time to go shopping, you'll have a whole bunch of great ideas ready and waiting.

- Use your handy list to keep track of the hints that your wife drops. If you hear her say, "I wish I had a necklace that matched this dress better," put it on the list!

- Don't be afraid to ask her friends. If you're shopping for the perfect necklace to go with the aforementioned dress, solicit help if you don't know your way around a jewelry department.

- Use your phone's camera when you're out shopping. If she points at a skirt she thinks is cute or an expensive brand of coffee she loves but wouldn't dream of indulging in, take a quick snapshot. Then head back to the store on your own and pick it up. She will be blown away by your thoughtfulness!

- If you're totally tapped for ideas, friends and family can be a terrific resource.

The last step in pro gift giving is to wrap it yourself before you give it to her. Don't tell her you didn't have time to wrap it or, worse, make her wrap it for you. Even if you are the worst wrapper in the world, it's an essential step and she will appreciate the extra effort.

Quickie 38:
The **worst** time to give the worst gift **ever**

The worst gift of all time is, ironically, one of the most commonly given.

Flowers. Bleeeech.

Oh sure, women like flowers well enough, but flowers are never a substitute for thoughtful gift giving. The only time you will ever get brownie points for giving your wife flowers is when they are a total surprise and/or you're giving them "just because." For example, you will win points by sending a bouquet to her office the morning of her big pitch meeting. You will win points by picking up some flowers on your way home from the guy on the corner just because their beauty reminded you of your wife.

Flowers on birthdays and anniversaries are appreciated, but you won't get any extra love for them. Flowers as the *only* gift on birthdays and anniversaries will actually cause you to lose a point or two (or ten). Why? Because they're overdone. They're impersonal. Throw a heart-shaped box of drugstore chocolates into the mix and you've got the ultimate boring, cliché, unimpressive present of all time.

The *worst* possible way for you to give flowers to your wife is after an argument. Contrary to what Hollywood would have you believe, flowers are not the ultimate cure-all – and the bigger the argument, the truer this is. When you give your wife "I'm sorry" flowers, all she hears from you is, "I think I can fix being a twit by bribing you." Not good. (One hubby we know thought he could halt his divorce proceedings with a dozen roses. Guess what? He's now an ex-hubby.)

In a similar vein, giving your wife flowers after she complains, "You're so unromantic, you don't even buy me flowers!" is really not a good idea. In female-speak, what she's saying is, "You're so unromantic, you don't even do the bare minimum." That's why, when you show up with a great big beautiful bouquet of the bare minimum, she's even madder than she was before. You've been warned.

To sum up:

- Flowers for no reason = good
- Flowers as a surprise = good
- Flowers accompanying a gift = acceptable
- Flowers for any other reason = danger!

Quickie 39:

Another pretty awful gift you should (**usually**) avoid like the plague

Greeting cards: they are a necessary evil, aren't they?

We say "necessary" because it's traditional to include a card with a gift. We say "evil" because it can be exhausting trying to find just the right one. Plus, depending on what you write in there, greeting cards can get you in a lot of hot water.

It only takes a few seconds to pick a random card off the shelf, pay for it, then write, "Love, Tom" inside. The lack of thought shines through so glaringly that your wife is guaranteed to hate it. And it only gets worse if, for some reason, all you are getting her is that card.

Avoid the pitfalls greeting cards cause by writing the words yourself. Sure, they might be less eloquent than what the professionals at the greeting card company wrote, but who cares? Your wife will appreciate your genuine thoughts. See if you're up for the challenge of picking a totally blank card, then filling it only with your thoughts! (Don't be surprised if she sheds a happy tear or two!)

So, you know you have to get her a card. You also know that you can't just let the card put words in your mouth. But there is one other thing you need to watch out for when it comes to greeting cards: the potentially cool, but very risky, greeting card gift.

A "greeting card gift" is when you give her something that can fit inside a greeting card envelope, like tickets to a play or a gift certificate for a massage. This can be fantastic, but you have to proceed with extreme caution if your greeting card gift is to take her shopping for her present. It's doable, but dangerous.

The way to set this up is to write in a sweet card, "Honey, I know you mentioned you wanted a new sweater. Let's go out this weekend and find one that you love!" Note that this works because (a) you have an idea in mind, (b) you have a plan to take her out, and (c) you are not going to complain even once while at the mall (right?). This idea will NOT work if you don't already have a gift idea in mind, if you never actually make good on your IOU (lamentably, this happens a lot), if you make her go shopping alone, or if you whine and complain the whole time you're out. The idea here is to convey "I know what you'd like but I want to make sure it's perfect," not "I had no idea what to get you so I just grabbed this dumb card and you can do the rest yourself." (Note: for tips on how to come up with awesome gift ideas, see Quickie 37).

EXTRA BROWNIE POINTS

If you're tech-savvy, try making her a card using a cute, sentimental photo. For maximum impact, choose a childhood pic of her celebrating the same occasion as the one you're now making the card for, or one from her first Mother's Day (ideal for a Mother's Day card, of course), or even a photo of the two of you when you were just dating (charming for anniversaries). She won't believe how adorable you are!

Quickie 40:
The secrets to planning **killer** special occasions

In the grand scheme of things, special occasions don't come up all that often. So, when they do come up, instead of stressing that you don't know what to do or what to buy, think of them as rare opportunities to really go all out in showing your wife how crazy you are about her.

Make a commitment right now to make every birthday, anniversary, Mother's Day, etc. special for your wife. Go out of your way to plan something extra special that will really "wow" her. Fortunately, it doesn't have to be that hard, as long as you allow yourself enough time so that you aren't trying to slap something together at the last minute. (Note: if you have one of those wives who says, "Oh, don't make a fuss for my birthday. I don't need anything," don't believe her! It's a trap!)

Here are some tips to put you on the right track for planning fabulous celebrations your wife will never forget:

- If you're taking her to a restaurant, choose it yourself (based on her preferences) and make the reservation. If you're taking her to a movie, choose a movie you know she wants to see. If you tell her you want to take her out but then make her pick the restaurant and the movie, she will be disappointed, even if you're just trying to make sure she gets what she wants for her big day. She wants *you* to handle the details so that she can just relax and be pampered.

- Handle getting the babysitter. Don't ask her to iron your shirt. Wrap her gift yourself. All women want to feel taken care of by their husbands. Handle all the details so she doesn't have to. If your plan for a special occasion creates extra work for her, she may resent it.

- Try to surprise her with something. Do something out of the ordinary. Dinner out is only going to impress her if you don't take her to the same old standby diner you use for your once-in-a-blue-moon date night. If you never cook for her, you can surprise her with an intimate, gourmet meal at home!

If this all seems like a lot of work, try to reframe your thinking. Take advantage of special occasions to show your wife you're paying attention and know her tastes. Remember that the more you put into these special occasions, the more you will get out of them – especially once the two of you have retired to the bedroom for the night.

STORY: FEEL FREE TO STEAL THESE AMAZING GUYS' IDEAS (THEY MADE US SWOON AND YOUR WIFE WILL TOO!)

Pay attention, guys! Here are a few stories of inspiration for planning perfect celebrations from husbands who really know how to knock special occasions out of the park:

For his wife's 40th birthday, one husband planned a surprise party with a murder mystery theme (which you can pick up at any store that sells board games). Parties with a theme, whether they are a surprise are not, are a great way to spice up the occasion. You could do a luau, a pool party, an '70s theme, a wine and cheese night... just think about what your wife is into and go from there.

Another very clever husband emailed all of his wife's girlfriends to say that his wife had been dropping hints that she wanted a new black purse for her birthday. He asked each one of them to pick out a purse (and keep the receipt just in case!) and bring it to his wife's party so she could choose her favorite. Then he reimbursed the woman who had brought the purse his wife loved most. So thoughtful (and next to no work for him)!

For Christmas one year, another husband did a "12 Days of Christmas" theme and got his wife 12 separate presents, one for each of the 12 days up to and including Christmas. Many of the presents were small and/or silly: for example, one gift was a new holiday tablecloth because their kids had colored all over their old one; another gift was several dozen shortbread cookies her hubby had baked so they would have some treats on hand for holiday visitors and gifts for the neighbors, mailman, etc. – without his wife having to do all the baking. The gift for Christmas Day? A gorgeous scarf that had caught her eye one day when they were out Christmas shopping. Amazing! Seriously, take a cue from this husband, guys!

Quickie 41:
Planning the **ultimate** romantic getaway

Whether it's at the bed and breakfast down the road or an elaborate trip overseas, it's pretty much a given that couples have more sex when they're able to unwind together on vacation.

To make the most of this golden opportunity, handle all of the details yourself. Your wife won't believe all the trouble you took to make this getaway special for the two of you! Here's what we're talking about:

- Make the reservations yourself, including travel, lodging, car rentals, whatever is needed.

- Research beforehand. Be sure to choose a place that is well rated. You want her to be surprised by how charming the accommodations are, not by the smell of stale smoke or foreboding stains on the carpet.

- Plan some activities at your destination. Figure out where the good restaurants are and sign the pair of you up for something fun, like a snorkeling excursion or a wine-tasting tour. Don't just get there, throw down your suitcase, and say to your wife, "Now what do you want to do?" Take charge!

- Handle the details back at home for the duration of your getaway, even if it's only overnight. Figure out who will look after your kids, pets, and plants. Put a hold on your mail. Enlist the help of a friend to come by and check on

the house every couple of days if you are going to be gone for an extended period of time. Ask your next-door neighbor to mow your lawn. All of this will put your wife's mind at ease so she can relax more and enjoy the romance of being alone with you.

● If the destination is a surprise, give your wife a mysterious packing list (for example, "Plan for bikinis by day and sundresses by night"). Although most women love surprises, they worry about the embarrassment of being underdressed or overdressed for the situation at hand. A packing list will be a tantalizing, teasing hint of what's to come, but it will also help her prepare so that she can actually enjoy herself.

Remember, your getaway doesn't have to be at a luxury resort or cost zillions of dollars to rekindle some romance in your marriage – so don't put off planning this special trip because of your finances. Even a simple day trip can get her juices flowing as long as you take the initiative and handle the details yourself. This is all about getting out of the everyday and pampering your wife, not about how much moolah you're shelling out to make it all happen.

Quickie 42:

Being **thoughtful** will get you in the **sack**

Women are pretty weird when it comes to their husbands' thoughtfulness. Maybe you have found yourself wondering why the tiniest gestures (like folding the clean laundry without being asked) seem to mean as much – or more – than the grander ones (like that show-stopping diamond tennis bracelet).

We're not sure if there truly is a logical explanation for this odd female tendency, but we're going to do our best to explain it to you. Basically, it's helpful to think not of the *size* of the gesture but of how much she will *expect* the gesture. This can help you understand why that pricey birthday gift didn't go over as well as the folded towels. In one case, she expected you to get her a gift; in the other case, you surprised her with your thoughtfulness.

In other words, you'll earn the most points with your wife when she least expects your thoughtfulness. So, yeah, if you've never been thoughtful, then you can count on your first few attempts to score pretty big – congratulations! You've got an unfair advantage over husbands who are routinely thoughtful with their wives. (Hey, we never said women are fair!)

Being thoughtful doesn't come naturally for a lot of guys, but the more you practice, the better you'll get. If your wife isn't feeling well, bring home some of her favorite soup and an assortment of cold medicine as a surprise. If she's been having a lot of trouble with your teenager lately, call her from work and ask her how things went that morning. For dinner, light some candles for no reason at all. Start with these small ideas and take it from there.

Do these ideas sound lackluster to you next to more extravagant gestures? Maybe so, but trust us when we say we can pretty much guarantee that any woman on the planet would go weak-kneed if her husband did these things for her. These are the kind of simple gestures that make your wife's friends say things like, "Awww! I am so jealous!" and "You have the best husband in the world!" That's the kind of husband you want to be.

Simple, thoughtful acts translate to big brownie points with your wife. Best of all, they take far less money, effort, and maddening time in shopping malls than fancier gestures. The sooner you can become the master of simple, thoughtful acts, the quicker your love life is going to be back on the upswing.

Quickie 43:
Sex – the **magic** number

How much sex is the right amount to be having in a given week? In a given month?

Sorry to say, but there is actually no magic number when it comes to how much sex you "should" be having. Every couple is different, and where you are in your relationship will also have a big impact on how often you're getting it on.

Figuring out what is the "right" amount of sex is tough because although the numbers vary widely from couple to couple, anecdotal evidence from your buddies or from what you see on TV is enough to make any guy feel like he's either inadequate or seriously missing out (or both!). If you're looking for some information that's actually based on fact, here are a few statistics that might surprise you:

- The average husband and wife only have sex 58 times per year, which is just barely over once a week.[ix]

- Within two years after saying "I do," about 20% of couples are having sex fewer than 10 times per year.[x]

- The negative impact of no sex on a marriage is much more significant than the positive impact of a fulfilled sex life.[xi]

So, if you're hoping to be having sex three times a week and you haven't been able to make it happen, know that three times a week is waaaaay above average and likely unrealistic for most couples. That said, it's true that happy couples *do* tend to have more sex than unhappy couples – it's just not as much as you think.

If your wife is perfectly happy only having sex once a week or every other week, trying to convince her that the two of you are "below average" is never going to amp up her sex drive. Instead, focus on being supportive and attentive if you want action in the sack – and if you're "only" getting it once a week or a couple of times a month, be glad you're not one of the 20% of couples who are only managing fewer than 10 times per year.

It's important to realize that how much sex other people are having is not a good barometer for your own sex life. Why? Because you have to figure out what works for the two of you as a couple, not what works for other people. If, however, you are really unhappy about your mismatched sex drives, have a candid conversation with your spouse and, if necessary, don't be shy about seeking the support of a therapist.

THE VIAGRA VICTIM STORY

Diane here! When I was still practicing as a litigation lawyer, I was working on a file in which a fellow claimed he no longer had the ability to get an erection due to the psychological impacts of an accident he'd been a victim of. As part of his compensation, he was making a claim for the cost of erectile dysfunction drugs based on his projected use of three times a week for the rest of his life.

I saw this in the file and looked up at my partner (a guy) with kind of an amused shock. "Wow!" I said. "Three times a week seems pretty optimistic, doesn't it?"

My partner nodded and whispered to me, "I thought so, too, but I was wondering if I was just an anomaly!"

The point is that perceptions about the frequency of sex are at best inaccurate and at worst destructive to our self-esteem *and* our sense of intimacy with our spouses. Instead of guessing what's best, be honest with yourself and your partner about what you want, then go from there.

Quickie 44:
The sex move that always **flops**

Picture this: You crawl into bed next to your wife, curl up behind her, and start nuzzling her neck. But before you can even round first base, she's already saying, "Not tonight" or "I have a headache" or "You know I have an early start tomorrow."

What gives? Well, one of the most common reasons women reject these advances is because by bedtime, they are too tired to even consider thinking about sex. She's just had a long day at work or chasing the kids, then scrambling to get dinner ready and cramming a few last-minute chores in before she flops into bed, exhausted. One thing that just didn't make her daily to-do list is sex with you.

Fortunately, a lot of the time you can help your wife get out of her head and into your arms simply by modifying your approach. You probably already know that, usually, it takes much longer for a woman to get turned on than for a man. So, instead of starting your foreplay once you're already both under the covers, get things simmering much earlier in the day.

Start by not giving your wife extra chores to do in the morning. Put your breakfast dishes in the dishwasher and hang up your towel. (For more on why chores are sexy, see Quickie 13.) Then, give her a passionate kiss before you leave for work and again when you come back home. During the day, send her a couple of flirty texts, telling her that you miss her or that you love the outfit she put on this morning.

Once you're home for the evening, try to give your wife some space to unwind – because a wound-tight woman is practically impossible to turn on. Bring her a glass of wine and hand her the remote while you tidy up after dinner. Volunteer to put the kids to bed while she takes a bath. Offer to give her a foot rub. When your wife has a chance to relax, her thoughts more naturally turn to snuggling up with you in bed later on.

The key thing to remember here is to start getting your wife in the mood waaaay before you've turned the lights out for the night. Although you might not think you're rushing her, if your very first moves are you caressing her back or kissing her earlobes in bed, your attempts will probably be in vain. If your wife is already thinking "sleep," it will be very difficult at that point to get her thinking "sex" – so give yourself a fighting chance by gently turning her thoughts to love-making by being sweet and sensual with her all day long.

Quickie 45:
Things **not** to **say** if you want to have sex

It's truly astounding how quickly the wrong choice of words can take your wife from "feeling frisky" to "totally turned off." If you say something that upsets or offends her, she can (and often will) withhold sex as a means of communicating her extreme displeasure.

You already know that if you say something stupid, you should apologize. However, we are all human and it's inevitable that you're going to say things at times that your wife will take the wrong way – whether it's because your words were hurtful or simply because she's in hormone-overdrive.

Either way, your best bet here is to avoid some common phrases that most wives hate. If you don't want to be in the doghouse, try not to say any of the following:

- "Relax, you're so uptight." (When you a tell a woman to relax, she hears you saying, "It's stupid that you're stressed out." Instead, ask what you can do to help.)

- "Why the sour face?" (Ouch! Try something more tactful, like, "I can tell something's on your mind. What happened?")

- "You're acting crazy!" or "You're acting like a child!" (Even if this is true, what do you accomplish by saying it? Hurtful comments like these will only serve to freeze you out of the bedroom indefinitely.)

- "Don't be so sensitive." (Newsflash: women *are* sensitive! Instead of being critical of her for it, be the superhero that defends and protects her feelings.)

- "I don't deserve this!" (If you're in a heated argument and your wife is being unfair, see if you can just keep quiet until she's done ranting. More often than not you will get an apology for her unkind words without you having to go on the defensive.)

- "Cheer up!" (This is like saying to your wife, "You have no right to be sad." Your wife should never have to justify her feelings. If she is sad, support her.)

- "You always see the worst in everything. Things really aren't that bad." (Any comment that contains a sweeping generalization like "always" or "never" is bound to piss your wife off.)

- "Not everything is all about you." (This is a pretty unkind thing to say.)

- "Hey, I think my mom is smart and beautiful, just like you!" (Never make comparisons between your wife and your mother, period.)

- "You're just jealous of my mom, admit it!" (Ditto.)

- "You're such a nag." (This is a serious button for literally every woman we know. Maybe she *is* nagging you needlessly, but then again, maybe there's a reason she's asking you to do something. Whatever you do, don't call her a nag.)

- "Don't get so defensive." (The quickest way to make your wife defensive is to accuse her of being defensive! Don't do it!)

- "Calm down. You're overreacting." (No one likes to hear that they're overreacting. Just ride it out.)

Quickie 46:
Your relationship bank account terms **suck**

Think of your marriage as a relationship bank account. Like a bank account, there are withdrawals and deposits. Every time you do something positive for your marriage, that counts as a deposit. Every time something negative happens, that's a withdrawal.

Unfortunately, the terms and conditions attached to this particular bank account are pretty darn crappy. For starters, your interest rate is practically nil. Deposits on your part will accrue a little bit of interest, but if they aren't followed up quickly with more deposits, then the steep monthly fees will more than eat away at your balance. In other words, you can't expect your positive actions to have an indefinitely positive effect on your marriage. You need to make regular contributions in order to keep your balance healthy.

In bank accounts and in marriages, it is inevitable that there will be some withdrawals as well as deposits. That's normal. What is important is for you to keep making deposits so that those withdrawals don't sting so much. When you have a healthy account, the occasional withdrawal is barely felt; but when your balance is low, withdrawals can cause all kinds of anxiety and upset. You have to be extra wary of withdrawals against a low balance because this is one bank that does not offer overdraft protection!

John Gottman, renowned relationship expert, has found that the "magic" ratio of positive to negative interactions for a marriage in conflict is 5:1.[xii] That means that for every negative interaction, there should be a bare minimum of five positive interactions in order for the marriage to remain on solid ground. This ratio is especially critical when your marriage is strained. A healthy, strong marriage may be able to sustain a period of less-than-optimal interaction ratios, but when the marriage is in trouble, maintaining the 5:1 balance can mean the difference between a marriage that grapples its way back to happiness and one that succumbs to divorce.

This book is filled with lots of tips and tricks to inspire your positive interactions and, hopefully, minimize the negative ones. The goal is for you to enjoy not just a healthier sex life, but also a happier marriage. As long as your relationship bank account is flush, it will be a lot easier for you to have both.

Quickie 47:
10-second sex tips

Think upping your game has to be time-consuming? Think again! Below are a whole bunch of 10-second tips that will bring you closer to your wife and, believe it or not, help restore some intimacy between the two of you:

Housework

- Hang up your towel.
- Wipe up any drips of water after having a shower.
- Throw your dirty clothes in the laundry hamper.
- Put the toilet seat down.
- Wipe up your "toilet splatter."
- Change the empty toilet paper roll.
- Wipe your whiskers out of the sink.
- Wipe your toothpaste splatter out of the sink.
- Put your dishes in the dishwasher/sink.
- Wipe down the table after a meal.
- Ask your wife what you can do to help out. (Yes, the resulting chore may take more than 10 seconds, but she will love you for asking.)

Appreciation

- Give her a hug.
- Kiss her passionately to say hello/goodbye.
- Take a photo of something she loves (so you can buy it later).

- Hold her hand.
- Pour her a glass of wine.
- Tell her one of the reasons you love her so much.
- Thank her for something specific (dinner, laundry, organizing, taking care of the kids, etc.)
- Send her a short love text (something simple like "You are beautiful!" or "Yummy soup – thanks!" is perfect).

Manners

- Open her car door for her, both when she's getting in and out.
- Open other doors for her, too!
- Say "please" and "thank you."
- Say "excuse me" when you burp, fart, or get up from the dinner table.
- Don't start eating until she sits down with you.
- When you're walking together, switch to the side of the sidewalk that's closer to traffic so that she feels better protected.

Communication

- Bite your tongue when you have the urge to make an excuse, get defensive, or lash out.
- When you want to give advice, ask a question instead.
- Validate her feelings (for example, "Wow, you definitely had a tough day" or, "I can see why what he said hurt you so much. That was unfair").

(Wondering how these 10-second tips translate into sex? Remember that your wife needs to feel loved, appreciated, and supported before she can feel turned on. You'll be amazed by what you can accomplish in your marriage with just 10 seconds of effort!)

Quickie 48:
One-minute sex tips

When you've got about 60 seconds to spare, try these tips to "wow" your wife in one minute flat (so that you'll have the chance to "wow" her later, under the covers):

Housework

- Put on a load of wash. Just make sure it's stuff you know how to launder (i.e. not her delicates).
- Wipe down the kitchen counters.
- Take out the garbage.
- Clean the bathroom sink.
- Clean the toilet seat and bowl.
- Dust something.

Appreciation

- Suggest a fun, romantic date night.
- Come up behind her while she's busy at the computer or preparing dinner and give her a little back rub.
- Set the table.
- Handwrite her a little love note and slip it into her briefcase, sock drawer, car, or wherever else she'll stumble across your sweet surprise.

Manners

- Drop her off at the door instead of making her walk from the car to wherever it is you're going. You'll get even more bonus points if it's raining! (Note: You can also do this when you're returning home. Let her wait inside while you go get the car.)

- Keep an umbrella in the car. After opening her door for her, protect her from the elements with the umbrella. What a gentleman!

- Remind yourself periodically to chew with your mouth closed, use your napkin, etc. – whatever are her usual dinner table pet peeves.

- At parties, check in with your wife often. She will appreciate that you want to be by her side.

- Take a minute to spruce yourself up before you go out. Change your shirt if it has a stain, check your breath, and comb your hair.

Communication

- Commit to listening to your wife when she is upset or stressed about something. Acknowledge that you hear what she's saying and understand her feelings by paraphrasing what you've heard.

- Instead of saying, "So, what did you do all day?" ask her specific questions like, "How were the kids for you today?" and "Did you get that call from the bank that you were expecting?" Specific questions like these tell your wife that you care about what's going on in her world.

Quickie 49:
10-minute sex tips

Got a little extra time on your hands? With just 10 spare minutes you can make a huge difference in the quality (and, by extension) intimacy of your marriage. Here are a few ideas:

Housework

- Put away your clean clothes (especially if she's the one who did the laundry).
- Fold whatever's in the dryer.
- Help out with the kids' bedtime routines.
- Help with cleanup after meals. Enlist your kids' assistance, too, so your wife can sit down and relax.
- Clean the shower/bathtub.
- Vacuum or sweep.
- Change a burnt-out light bulb.
- Choose a chore and dedicate 10 minutes to it. Yup, chores are booooring, but you'd be amazed at what you can get done in 10 measly minutes!

Appreciation

- Help out with dinner preparation when you get home. It only takes 10 minutes to make a salad or transfer dishes from their pots to servingware. Just ask your wife and she will point you in the right direction. If she says she doesn't need your help, don't flop down on the sofa. Set the table or get a head start on the dinner dishes.
- Go get her car washed.

- Put gas in her car.
- Make a small detour on the way home to pick up a surprise: flowers, dessert, or an "I love you" card.
- Plan a simple date and take care of the details: reservations, movie selection, babysitter, etc. Don't ask your wife for help.
- Get something done off your "honey-do" list.
- Give her a foot rub.
- Draw her a bath complete with candles, bubbles, and music.

Manners

- Be polite with other people. Your wife may get embarrassed if you bring up contentious or sensitive topics at parties or family gatherings.
- Control yourself when drinking. Don't go overboard. The last thing you want is your wife having to apologize for your embarrassing behavior.
- Drive more slowly if your wife is uncomfortable. It will take you an extra few minutes to get there, but there will be no marital tension to contend with.
- Control your road rage (if you have any) while your wife is in the car. She hates to see you so angry!
- Take 10 minutes to clean up your appearance when you're going out on dates or for special occasions. Shave, choose a nice outfit, spritz on cologne she loves, and make sure your breath smells minty-fresh.

Communication

- Listen to your wife's rants. The better you are paying attention, the shorter the rants will be.

- Side with your wife. When she is complaining about something, acknowledge her right to feel the way she feels.

- Reminisce with her. Sit on the couch and have a nice conversation. Talking is the ultimate foreplay for many women!

Quickie 50:
Foreplay takes time

How often have women complained to you that you rush through foreplay? We can honestly say that, from a female point of view, we have *never* heard a woman complain that her man is too leisurely with foreplay (but we've heard plenty of complaints to the opposite effect!).

But this Quickie isn't actually about foreplay. It's about "foreplay," by which we mean the time you spend with your wife that leads up to sex. *But wait,* you're probably thinking, *isn't that what foreplay is?*

Yes, but we want you to think about foreplay on a larger scale… not just when you curl up next to her in bed, but all day long or even all week long, from when you wish her good luck with her Monday PTA meeting to when you plan a romantic date for Saturday night, sans kids.

Is stuff like that really foreplay? To you it might not be, but to her, it definitely is. As you've undoubtedly noticed, it can take a *lot* of time to turn a woman on. But when she's feeling closer to you because of how thoughtful and appreciative you've been, it's much easier for her to get in touch with herself (and, consequently, you) sexually. Maybe it will take a few extra hours or maybe it will take several weeks.

Weeks?!? you might be thinking with dismay. Well, just like foreplay takes time, you need to appreciate that your efforts may take time to sink in. It's not realistic to unload the dishwasher one time and then expect your wife to drop her drawers and make love to you right there on the kitchen floor. It will take time for her to feel appreciated, admired, respected and – yes – turned on. Hang in there – you are in this for the long haul.

Taking your time is also important because you want your wife to understand the motivation behind the changes you're making. You don't want to make her think that you're only doing these things because you want to get into her pants. If she thinks that, it will cheapen all of your hard work and your efforts will very likely backfire. Then your investment of time and energy will be for nothing! Instead, be patient. Give your wife time to appreciate what you're doing and for that appreciation to blossom into a busier sex life.

At first, your wife may not know what to make of the changes you've made recently. She might even think you did something wrong and are trying to make it up to her! But gradually, she will eventually notice and appreciate all of the sweet things you're doing. You just need to keep at it. A happier wife – and the resulting fringe benefits – are more than worth the effort. Best of luck!

Endnotes

[i] Gray, J. (1992). *Men Are From Mars, Women Are From Venus.* New York, NY: HarperCollins Publishers.

[ii] Chapman, G. D. (1992). *The Five Love Languages: the Secret to Love That Lasts.* Chicago, IL: Northfield Publishing.

[iii] Gottman, J.M. & Silver, N. (1999). *The Seven Principles for Making Marriage Work.* New York, NY: Three Rivers Press.

[iv] Sandberg, S. (2010, December). *Why We Have too few Women Leaders.* Speech presented at TEDWomen, Washington, D.C. Retrieved from http://www.ted.com/talks/ sheryl_sandberg_why_we_have_too_few_women_leaders.html

[v] Study: Women Find Men Who Do Housework Sexy. (2003). ABC News. Retrieved from http://abcnews.go.com/GMA/ WaterCooler/story?id=124720&page=1

[vi] Harrar, S. & DeMaria, R.M. (2006). *The 7 Stages of Marriage: Laughter, Intimacy, and Passion, Today, Tomorrow, Forever.* Pleasantville, NY: Reader's Digest.

[vii] Gottman, J.M. & Silver, N. (1999). *The Seven Principles for Making Marriage Work.* New York, NY: Three Rivers Press.

[viii] "Romance." (2005) *The New Oxford American Dictionary.* New York, NY: Oxford University Press.

[ix] Parker-Pope, T. (2009, June 3). When Sex Leaves the Marriage. The New York Times. Retrieved from well.blogs.nytimes.com/ 2009/06/03/when-sex-leaves-the-marriage/

[x] Harrar, S. & DeMaria, R.M. (2006). *The 7 Stages of Marriage: Laughter, Intimacy, and Passion, Today, Tomorrow, Forever.* Pleasantville, NY: Reader's Digest.

[xi] Gottman, J.M. & Schwartz Gottman, J. (2006). *10 Lessons to Transform Your Marriage*. New York, NY: Three Rivers Press.

[xii] Gottman, J.M. (1994). *What Predicts Divorce? The Relationship Between Marital Processes and Marital Outcomes*. Hillsdale, NJ: Lawrence Erlbaum Associates.

Made in the USA
Charleston, SC
10 December 2013